ngc

CO-041 S

FROGS & TOADS

A COMPLETE INTRODUCTION

The wood frog of North America, Rana sylvatica, *is a striking and often common species.*

This tropical tree frog, *Agalychnis annae*, is most suitable for the advanced hobbyist.

FROGS & TOADS

A COMPLETE INTRODUCTION

Green toads, Bufo viridis, are one of the most colorful European species but are now considered threatened.

Jay Pyrom

Photography:
M. Auber-Thomay; Dr. Herbert R. Axelrod; Dr. Warren E. Burgess; George Dibley; Dr. Guido Dingerkus; F. J. Dodd, Jr.; John Dommers; Michael Gilroy; R. Haas; H. Hansen; Burkhard Kahl; J. K. Langhammer; F. Letellier; Ken Lucas, Steinhart Aquarium; W. Mudrack; K. T. Nemuras; Aaron Norman; Ivan Sazima; P. W. Scott; Dr. D. Terver, Nancy Aqu., France; Ruda Zukal.

46922)
(w) 639.378 7?

Distributed in the UNITED STATES by T.F.H. Publications, Inc., 211 West Sylvania Avenue, Neptune City, NJ 07753; in CANADA to the Pet Trade by H & L Pet Supplies Inc., 27 Kingston Crescent, Kitchener, Ontario N2B 2T6; Rolf C. Hagen Ltd., 3225 Sartelon Street, Montreal 382 Quebec; in CANADA to the Book Trade by Macmillan of Canada (A Division of Canada Publishing Corporation), 164 Commander Boulevard, Agincourt, Ontario M1S 3C7; in ENGLAND by T.F.H. Publications Limited, 4 Kier Park, Ascot, Berkshire SL5 7DS; in AUSTRALIA AND THE SOUTH PACIFIC by T.F.H. (Australia) Pty. Ltd., Box 149, Brookvale 2100 N.S.W., Australia; in NEW ZEALAND by Ross Haines & Son, Ltd., 18 Monmouth Street, Grey Lynn, Auckland 2 New Zealand; in SINGAPORE AND MALAYSIA by MPH Distributors (S) Pte., Ltd., 601 Sims Drive, #03/07/21, Singapore 1438; in the PHILIPPINES by Bio-Research, 5 Lippay Street, San Lorenzo Village, Makati Rizal; in SOUTH AFRICA by Multipet Pty. Ltd., 30 Turners Avenue, Durban 4001. Published by T.F.H. Publications Inc. Manufactured in the United States of America by T.F.H. Publications, Inc.

Contents

Introduction

People have mixed feelings about frogs and toads; some shudder at the very thought of them, some eat them, others find them charming. It is to this latter group of sensible and forward-thinking people that this little book is dedicated.

For generations, man has had the urge to keep things in cages or tanks for the sake of curiosity, but it is only in the last few decades, as he has moved further and further from nature, that the desire to possess a small facsimile of a natural habitat in the home has reached almost epidemic proportions. To many city dwellers, opportunities to visit the countryside may be few and far between. Apart from occasional tantalizing glimpses of wildlife on the television screen, the only way they are going to have regular contact with fascinating wild creatures is to keep them on their own property. This may take the form of an aviary in the garden containing exotic birds; a fish pond decorated with aquatic plants and colorful goldfish; an indoor aquarium containing gem-like tropical fish; or a terrarium containing terrestrial animals of one form or another.

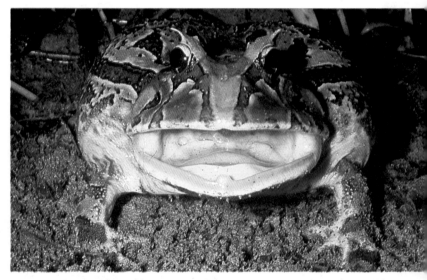

Due to their relatively small size, their attractive or bizarre appearance, and their interesting habits, frogs and toads have recently increased in popularity as household pets. An advantage of keeping these creatures is that they require almost natural conditions in which to live, which gives one the opportunity to create a miniature natural habitat, complete with its pond, its plants, and the amphibians themselves, that forms an ideal centerpiece in the living room or den. Given a few basic requirements and a few minutes each day, it is easy to keep an exhibit of these animals, providing the ongoing enthusiasm remains.

The following text introduces the beginner to the fascinating world of frogs and toads and gives concise guidelines on obtaining, housing, feeding, and caring for these charming creatures. It is hoped that this book will lead the enthusiast into years of pleasure and entertainment from what must surely be one of the most interesting of all hobbies.

Evolution and Classification

Whatever kind of animal the enthusiast wishes to keep in the home, it is interesting to know a little about the background of the creature in question. Not only does this give one a better "feel" for the little captives, but it gains one greater respect from one's contemporaries. This chapter is dedicated to information that is not strictly necessary to enable one to successfully keep frogs and toads in captivity, but it is thought that such information will greatly enhance the interest of the beginner who desires to know more about these creatures.

Evolution of the Amphibia

Frogs and toads belong to the animal class Amphibia, extinct members of which were the first vertebrates (backboned animals) to colonize the dry land that had hitherto been the domain of terrestrial plants and certain invertebrates, notably some early insects. The only previous vertebrates on earth at the time had been classes of fishes that were totally adapted to an aquatic existence. As numerous different species of fishes evolved, competition grew rapidly and, in some cases, bodies of water gradually began to dry up. For these two reasons certain groups of fishes, notably the lungfishes (three genera of which live at the present time) and the crossopterygian or lobe-finned fishes (the only living representative being the coelacanth), developed means of respiring atmospheric oxygen rather than extracting oxygen from the water using gills as was the method used by most other fish species. Over periods of

Facing page: *A tropical horned frog,* Ceratophrys aurita.

Woodhouse's toad, Bufo woodhousei, *is excellent for beginners.*

millions of years primitive lungs developed, enabling these fishes to survive in waters not suitable for more conventional species. They were even able to survive for prolonged periods in areas where the water had all but dried up.

Toward the end of the Devonian period, some 350 million years ago, some of the crossopterygian fishes came out on the land. It is very likely that these were of a type represented by the genus *Eusthenopteron*. In evolutionary terms this was one of the boldest steps in history: a venturing of early vertebrates into a completely new environment to which they were only partially adapted. Once this step had been made, however, it was not long before these advanced, air-breathing fishes became transformed into primitive amphibians. From available fossil evidence it can be surmised that the earliest amphibians belonged to a group known as ichthyostegids, creatures that had

Triprion spatulata, *one of the most bizarre tropical tree frogs.*

characteristics intermediate between crossopterygian fishes and the later true amphibians.

A typical ichthyostegid, *Ichthyostega*, had a skull about 15 cm (6 in) in length. Although similar in many respects to the skull of the crossopterygian fishes, there were changes in proportion between that of the fish and that of the amphibian. In the fish, for example, the part of the skull in front of the eyes was comparatively short and the portion of the skull behind the eyes was comparatively long. In *Ichthyostega* the reverse situation prevailed, in that the portion of the skull behind the eyes was relatively shorter than that of the fishes and the portion in front relatively longer. In the true amphibians the eyes tended to be oriented more toward the top of the skull than in the fishes. Although *Ichthyostega* had developed strong pectoral and pelvic girdles that carried completely developed limbs and

feet, the fin rays of the fish tail were retained. From this early fish/amphibian we can follow the evolution of the later amphibians as they radiated into various lines.

In changing from a life in water to a life on land, various problems had to be resolved. While a fish normally obtains its oxygen from water by means of gills, the early

One of the few caecilians likely to be seen by hobbyists, the aquatic Typhlonectes natans *from South America.*

amphibians had to further develop and perfect the lungs that they had inherited from their crossopterygian ancestors, although in the larval stages (as is still the case with modern amphibians) they continued to respire by means of gills. Another problem that land-dwelling animals had to contend with was desiccation or drying up. To the fish this is no problem as it is continually bathed by the liquid in which it lives, but to land-dwelling creatures it is a major problem. The amphibians are faced with the necessity of retaining their body fluids while no longer immersed in water. It can be surmised that the earliest amphibians, such as *Ichthyostega*, never ventured very far away from lakes and rivers to which they returned at frequent intervals, a habit that has followed through to today's modern amphibians. Certain branches of these early amphibians developed more and more efficient ways of conserving body fluids and became the precursors of the reptiles, from which the birds and the mammals ultimately arose.

Another problem that arises from a life on land is the influence of gravity. Whereas fishes are supported by the dense water in which they live and have developed a system of locomotion through body movements and fin stability, the first land-dwelling vertebrates had to evolve a system of moving over the land and supporting the body in the relatively thin atmosphere. Therefore, a strong backbone and sturdy limbs were developed in the earliest stages of their evolution. The vertebral column was supported by a pectoral girdle at the front (which in turn was supported by the arms and the hands) and a pelvic girdle at the rear part of the body (which was supported by the legs and the feet). These limbs served not only to support the body against gravitational pull, but were the means by which the animal could propel itself over the land surface. The early amphibians retained a tail, which probably functioned as an organ of balance. In addition,

The skeleton of a common green frog. Bone is shown in red, cartilage in blue.

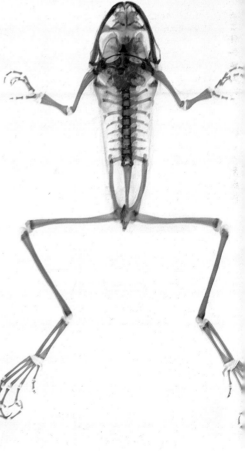

Evolution and Classification

the tail could still be used as an organ of propulsion when the amphibian returned to a watery environment. Although amphibians made a major contribution to life on land, they never solved the problem of terrestrial reproduction. Throughout their history these animals have had to return to water or (in some specialized forms) to damp areas in order to lay their eggs.

From the original ichthyostegids a number of lines evolved that not only eventually led to our modern amphibians but also radiated into the ancestral lines of reptiles, birds, and mammals. Most of the earlier amphibians were large salamander-like creatures, including the lepospondyles—from which the lines leading to modern caecilians and urodeles developed—and the labyrinthodonts—from which the line leading to modern anurans (frogs and toads) developed. (Some researchers believe that all modern amphibians evolved from the same ancestor rather than two distinct lineages.) A large gap in geological time separates the lepospondyles and the labyrinthodonts from the modern salamanders and frogs, but the

first frog-like creatures appeared in the early Triassic period about 225 million years ago. A great deal of evolutionary change must have taken place in order to produce a frog, which was anatomically very different from the early salamander-like amphibians. The only fossil frog that so far has shown evidence of ancestry from the earlier amphibians is *Triadobatrachus* from the early Triassic of Madagascar. This amphibian had a relatively short body with a mere remnant of a tail, and the limbs had already taken on characteristics typical of modern frogs and toads. From Jurassic times on (in the last 190 million years), frogs and toads have been characterized by an open, flat skull, by a short backbone (vertebrae reduced to about eight), by greatly elongated hind legs and short front legs, and by the total loss of the tail in the adult.

Classification
There are about 4000 known species of amphibians living on

The red-backed salamander, Plethodon cinereus, *is a typical salamander.*

earth today, most of which are frogs and toads. When one takes into consideration the total number of all types of animals and plants, it is not surprising that a certain amount of confusion existed (and may well still do so in certain cases) among scientists endeavoring to sort out the species into some kind of logical system. Fortunately, a system was developed that has solved the vast majority of problems, this being known as the *binomial* system of scientific nomenclature, in which each distinct species (the most natural and basic group, consisting of individuals that are very similar and freely interbreed) is awarded a double scientific name. The system was pioneered by the Swedish biologist Carl von Linné (1707-1778), generally known as Linnaeus. Basically, the system dictated that each species described to science should be given a generic and a specific name. As an example, the North American bullfrog is known scientifically as *Rana catesbeiana*, the first name being that of the genus, the second that of the species. There are many other species of the genus *Rana* (*Rana temporaria, Rana ridibunda, Rana dalmatina*, and so on), but all of these species show certain similarities that warrant them being placed in the same genus.

Genera (plural of genus) are grouped into larger categories in ascending sequence—the family, the order, the class and so on. Each level of classification is based on similarities or differences in the various groups. To illustrate the situation clearly, the following table shows the classification of a single species of frog, the spring peeper, *Hyla crucifer*.

Kingdom: Animalia—All animals
Phylum: Chordata—All chordates
Subphylum: Vertebrata—All vertebrates
Superclass: Tetrapoda—Limbed vertebrates
Class: Amphibia—All amphibians
Order: Anura—Frogs and toads
Family: Hylidae—Various tree frogs and their relatives
Genus: *Hyla*—Tree frogs
Species: *Hyla crucifer*—Spring peeper
Subspecies: *H. c. crucifer*—Northern spring peeper; *H. c. bartramiana*—Southern spring peeper

Hyla crucifer, the spring peeper, is one of the most common eastern American frogs.

It will be seen in the table that the typical species of tree frog chosen as an example is *Hyla crucifer*. This species was selected because two subspecies have been described for it. In cases where geographical races are slightly different but not

13

different enough to warrant separate specific rank, a subspecific name is added to the binomial. In such cases the first described population of the species represents the nominate subspecies and has its specific name simply repeated, thus: *Hyla crucifer crucifer* (or more conveniently *H. c. crucifer*). Further races described will receive a different subspecific name, thus: *H. c. bartramiana*. Subspecies will freely interbreed with each other where their natural ranges overlap or when they are brought together in captive conditions. Such intersubspecific hybrids are

Latin and Greek, as these were the languages universally used by learned scholars at the time of the inception of the binomial system. To the modern frog fancier it may seem rather superfluous to bother to learn Latin names of the various species when there are perfectly good English ones to use. However, by using Latin names we can not only overcome the boundaries of language (scientific names being universal), we can also overcome the problems of a species being given a different common name in the same and different languages. For example, *Bufo bufo* is called Erdkröte

Some species of frogs can come in many colors.

known as intergrades, which may resemble either of the parents, may have the characteristics of both, or may sometimes have a totally different appearance. Natural intergrades frequently pose taxonomic problems to field researchers.

In normal literature, the generic, specific, and subspecific names are universally italicized (or underlined in the absence of italic script). Most scientific names are derived from classical

("earth toad") in Germany, just toad or common toad in England, while in the USA it is called the European toad. It cannot be called the common toad in the USA as it is certainly not common there, being replaced by other species. It is therefore highly recommended that anyone who wants to make a hobby of keeping or studying frogs and toads should make an effort to learn a little about their classification.

Biology of Frogs and Toads

The life history of the average frog is known by every school child. Frogs have for a long time been standard equipment in the teaching of biology, both from the viewpoint of reproductive as well as anatomical studies. For some reason (perhaps on account of availability) the poor frogs have been decimated in their millions by students cutting them up on the laboratory bench, examining their insides, and passing electrical currents through their severed limbs. In this book we are less concerned about the internal anatomy of the anurans than with their behavioral biology. (Anura, by the way, means literally "no tail," thus its applicability to frogs and toads as opposed to salamanders.) In order to keep them alive in our terraria, it is most important that we know what makes them tick and what influences their breeding cycles.

Frog Versus Toad
Let us first endeavor to explain the differences between "frogs" and "toads." The two words originated in England, where the slippery types were given the word *frog* and the dry-skinned, warty types were termed *toads*. In other words, members of the genus *Rana* are frogs, and members of the genus *Bufo* are toads. This is rather unfortunate as, with the advent of world exploration, many further genera were described, some of which fit into neither category. In fact, members of the genus *Hyla* are normally termed *tree frogs*, but they are more closely related to the bufonids than the ranids. To get around this problem, the frog experts call all tailless amphibians *anurans* (members of the order Anura) or just uses frog in a general sense to include toads as well.

Typical Life History
The typical breeding season starts at a suitable time of the year, usually triggered by

Hyla pulchella, a rough-skinned Amazonian tree frog.

15

Biology of Frogs and Toads

favorable changes in climatic conditions, such as rising temperatures and/or an increase in photoperiod (length of daylight) in temperate and subtropical areas, the beginning of the rainy season in tropical rain forest areas, or only after heavy rains in arid areas (in the latter situation anuran species are adapted to complete their breeding cycle in a relatively short period, before the water dries up again). Taking the common European frog, *Rana temporaria*, as an example, the male frogs congregate in a suitable pond or slow-moving water course in early spring, having been awakened from their hibernation by the slight increase in temperature. Although not one of the more vocal anuran species, *R. temporaria* males emit a quiet croak that comes in two pitches, one of which is designed to attract female frogs, the other to repel over-amorous males. The females arrive at the water somewhat later. There is usually considerable jostling among the males (which often outnumber the females by as many as three to one) to gain the attentions of a female. Eventually each female will be grasped by a male around the body behind the forelimbs in a characteristic embrace known as *amplexus*. The grip is very strong

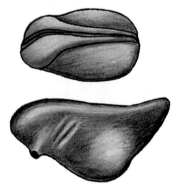

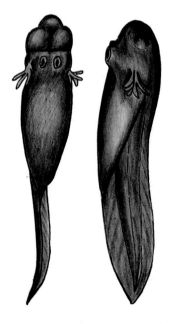

Eggs, early embryos, and early tadpoles of a leopard frog.

and is aided by nuptial pads, roughened dark areas on the thumbs of breeding males. This stimulates the female to lay her eggs, which may number up to 2000. As the eggs are being laid, a stream of sperm is shed by the male to fertilize them.

The eggs are laid in thick clumps of a hundred or more and rapidly absorb water, forming a transparent jelly-like protective capsule. Each individual egg is globular, black, and about 2-3 mm (1/8 in) in diameter, the capsule up to 8 mm (3/8 in). After laying, the parents take no further interest in the eggs and eventually leave the water. In a few days the eggs will hatch and the larvae (tadpoles) will first attach themselves to the jelly for a day or two while absorbing the remainder of the yolk sac from which they derive nourishment. Soon they take on the well-known tadpole form and become free-swimming. In the initial stages they will feed on algae, which they remove from plants and other surfaces with their rasping jaws. As they grow their appetite increases and they will begin to take animal matter ranging from tiny invertebrates to carrion. The hind legs appear first, followed by the front limbs a few days later. The appetite diminishes temporarily as the tail is absorbed and the little froglet prepares to leave the water for its first experience at terrestrial life. The common European frog spends most of its time on land, where it hunts for insects and other invertebrates in damp grassland, wooded areas, and meadows not too far from water. It returns to the water only to breed or to hibernate in the mud at the bottom of some pond.

Variations in Life History
Thus we have a brief summary of the life of a "typical" species. However, of the 4000 or so species of anurans known to science (and new species still being discovered fairly frequently), many have life histories and habits that are far from typical. Frogs have radiated into some amazingly diverse habitats, ranging from the tops of forest trees to arid deserts and from the edge of the Arctic to the peaks of mountains. Often the method of reproduction reflects the habitat. There are many tropical tree-dwelling species that lay a small number of eggs in a water-filled hollow in a tree branch or in the water store of a

Early and late tadpoles of a leopard frog.

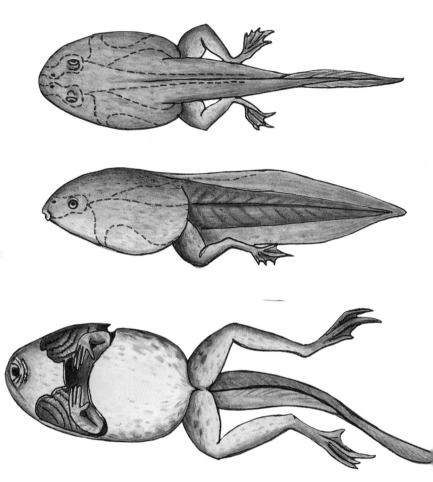

Very large tadpoles of a leopard frog, showing the hind legs and the front legs developing.

bromeliad, pitcher plant, or other similar place. In some species parental care is highly developed to the extent that adults transport the eggs or the tadpoles around on their backs. Other tropical species build a foam nest on the end of a tree branch overhanging the body of water into which the tadpoles drop when they hatch. There is even a "marsupial frog" in which the larvae metamorphose in a pouch on the back of the female.

Feeding
All adult anurans are carnivorous, actively hunting invertebrates of a size they can easily overpower. Most species possess a sticky, protrusible tongue that they can shoot out at remarkable speed to catch some unwary insect. The eye sockets are mobile and may be used to help force bulky items of food into the gullet. Some aquatic genera lack such a

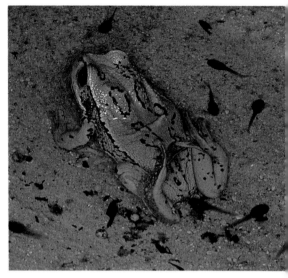

A female marsupial frog, Gastrotheca, *releasing its tadpoles.*

tongue and catch their prey by simply gulping it down. Some of the larger species can swallow amazingly large items, including small birds, mammals, and even each other!

Calls

The calls of frog species have an amazing variety, ranging from bird-like trills to deep, cattle-like bellows and from rapid staccato croaks to long, drawn out moans. Each species has its own pattern of calling, and scientists are able to recognize different species (which may be externally almost identical in color and form) by their call alone. Recordings of frog calls are a valuable aid in gathering data on distribution of species without even having to capture or examine the amphibian itself.

Variation in vocal sacs, a leopard frog above and a tree frog below.

Housing

Having decided to keep frogs and/or toads in the home, the first step before any animals are acquired is to ensure that adequate accommodations are available. The keeping of any animal in captivity is an undertaking of considerable responsibility, and unless you are sure that you have the necessary time and devotion to the hobby, then you should never start in the first place. The type of housing required will differ from species to species depending on whether they are totally aquatic, semiaquatic, terrestrial, or arboreal. A container in which living animals (and plants) are kept is called a vivarium or terrarium for terrestrial creatures, an aquarium for aquatic creatures. For creatures that are partly terrestrial and partly aquatic, an aqua-terrarium is used. Being amphibious, one would imagine that anurans should be kept in aquaria or aqua-terraria, but this is not always the case. Before deciding on a species, ensure that you have a knowledge of its habits and native habitat so that you can provide conditions as nearly natural as possible. Where it is impossible to produce conditions that are totally natural, some acceptable compromise situations can usually be produced.

The Aquarium

In this context we are referring to the aquarium as a container of water reproducing a totally aquatic environment with no exposed land areas. Aquarium tanks may also be used as other types of housing. There are many kinds of aquarium tanks available on the market, including molded clear plastic or plexiglass tanks that are usually small and ideal for rearing tadpoles or young anurans. One disadvantage of such plastic tanks is that after continued use and cleaning a film of fine scratches will eventually spoil the view into the vessel. Another type of aquarium is the old-fashioned iron-framed type in which sheets of glass are fixed with putty in a steel frame. The disadvantages of these tanks are that unless the frames are rust-proofed and painted at regular intervals with non-toxic paint they will rust away. In addition, traditional putty tends to shrink and crack if the tank is stored empty of water.

Without doubt, the finest type of aquarium tank available on the market today is the all-glass tank. This consists of a number of sheets of glass of appropriate sizes cemented together along their edges with a remarkably versatile substance called silicone rubber sealing compound. It is possible to purchase such

Water surfaces can be built into the bottom of the tank or a simple water bowl provided instead.

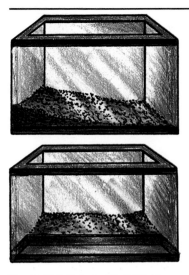

The basic terrarium can easily be made from an old aquarium.

the front of the tank, sloping to about 7.5 cm (3 in) at the rear, should be placed in the aquarium base. Non-toxic rocks (granite, slate, etc., but not limestone) may be placed to form valleys, caves, and terraces. Various aquatic plants may be planted in the substrate (you may require additional fertilizing materials; ask at your pet shop), usually with the smaller ones at the front, grading to the largest at the back and ends. Larger frogs are quite violent with the substrate and will continually uproot weak plants, so only robust plants should be used, these being allowed to become established before the frogs are introduced. Such aquaria are suitable for rearing tadpoles or keeping totally aquatic frogs such as *Xenopus*, *Hymenochirus*, and *Pipa*.

aquaria ready-made or have one made to your specifications.

Care should be taken in positioning an aquarium for aquatic anurans. A sturdy base should be chosen (remembering that a tank full of water is extremely heavy) and preferably placed away from a window. Once in its permanent position, the tank should be thoroughly cleaned and then filled with water and tested for leaks, which can be repaired with the same sealing compound.

Substrate Material
Most of the smaller aquatic frogs will appreciate a natural looking environment with plants, rocks, and other decorative materials. Good tips on setting up a planted aquarium may be obtained from books about tropical or cold-water fish. Here it will suffice to say that a layer of aquarium gravel about 5 cm (2 in) deep at

The Aqua-Terrarium
The aqua-terrarium is one that is roughly half land and half water. Such containers are suited for anurans that like to spend equal amounts of time in the water and on the land. They are also suited for breeding quarters for many species and are ideal for rearing tadpoles to the adult stage. An ordinary aquarium tank can be used with a partition of glass about 15 cm (6 in) high cemented across the bottom of the tank to make a waterproof barrier between the land and water areas. The substrate of the water area can be about 2.5 cm (1 in) deep, this giving a water depth of 12.5 cm (5 in). A rock gradient can be placed up the side of the glass partition so that the inmates can easily enter and leave the water. The land area is filled to about half with pebbles and coarse gravel to provide drainage, then a mixture of

Housing

Hyla squirella, *the squirrel tree frog.*

frame and above that a frame of fine mesh or gauze can be added. With careful artistic planning it is possible to create a really natural looking micro-habitat complete with a waterfall and tropical rain forest plants. Such a display will be ideal for many tropical species, which should breed readily in the water provided. One word of caution: after using cement, fill the tank with water and leave for 24 hours, then drain and scrub the cement surfaces. This should be done three or four times, until lime deposits (seen as a whitish film on the surface of the cement) and chemical smells are no longer apparent.

garden loam, peat, and clean sand is added on top. The mixture should preferably be sterilized to reduce the possibility of the soil souring and becoming moldy. A slab of turf can be placed over the whole area (this can be changed at regular intervals) or clumps of moss can be used. One or two dwarf potted plants can be sunk into the substrate, and mossy bark, stone caves, or broken plant pots can be used as hiding places for the inmates.

A more ambitious and natural looking aqua-terrarium can be made by using a very large tank and building a rockery up from the rear in an alcove in the house or conservatory. In this case the whole of the aquarium tank becomes the pond, and the back wall is built up with natural rocks and cement to form a false river bank. Cavities left between the rocks can be filled with potting compost. Various semiaquatic plants may be installed in the bank area. The front of the display above the aquarium tank can be filled in with a sheet of glass in a

The Tall Terrarium

The tall terrarium is one that is specially constructed for species of arboreal (tree-dwelling) frogs that do not require large bodies of water in which to breed (*Dendrobates* species, for example). Such terraria may consist of a glass-fronted wooden box, but as a high humidity will be

Coarse gravel is probably the most common substrate.

Arboreal frogs, such as the Malayan flying frogs, Rhacophorus, *need tall terraria.*

required, it is best to have a specially made all-glass tank. This should be taller than its width. A suitable size for a pair of small frogs is 50 x 50 x 75 cm tall (20 x 20 x 30 in). The base of the tank can be given a layer of gravel about 2.5 cm (1 in) thick, and this may be covered with slabs of moss. A dead tree branch is placed in the center. This can be decorated with living epiphytic plants, especially bromeliads of the type that hold water in their bracts. Certain species of frog will hide in the bracts and will even breed in them.

Life-support Systems
As well as the basic tank and its decorations, there are a number of life-support systems that are essential to the inmates. These include heating, lighting, humidity control, ventilation, and filtration. All of these systems warrant discussion in some detail.

The Terrarium Lid: The terrarium lid not only prevents the inmates from escaping, it forms housing for the lighting system (and possibly the heating) and

provides ventilation. A terrarium lid is usually made from plastic but can be made from plywood given a couple of coats of non-toxic gloss paint to make it damp-proof. A couple of large holes are made in the top of the lid and these are covered with fine gauge mesh. The lid should be at least 15 cm (6 in) deep to allow for lighting apparatus.

Ololygon species, one of the multitude of Amazonian tree frogs.

Housing

Heating: Anurans from temperate climates will require little if any supplementary heating, but most tropical species will, of course, require temperatures that are normally higher than those prevailing in most European and North American areas. As the majority of amphibians require reasonably high humidity, it is best to use equipment that will provide both warmth and humidity. One of the most satisfactory ways of heating small terraria is to use aquarium heaters of the type supplied for tropical fish tanks. There are many kinds available on the market, and it is advisable to visit your local pet shop to see what is most suitable to your setup.

Most aquarium heaters consist of an element in a heat-resistant waterproof glass tube. A thermostat may be present in the same tube or it may come in a separate tube. A thermostat is, however, an essential part of the equipment. In the aqua-terrarium, the heater is simply placed in the water. This will often be sufficient (particularly in association with the lighting) to provide a satisfactory range of temperatures (most tropical anurans require a temperature in the range of 23-30°C [73-86°F]). As the water is heated, slow evaporation takes place that will increase and maintain the humidity in the air. In the terrarium that contains no large areas of water (as in the tall tree frog terrarium) the aquarium heater may simply be placed in a concealed jar of water situated in

Because Bombina orientalis *comes from cool Asian streams, it can do without supplemental heating.*

Rana limnocharis *from southern Asia needs warm water.*

Standard aquarium heaters are satisfactory for many terrarium situations.

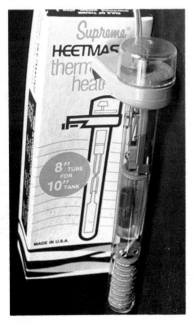

the rear of the tank.

Other forms of heating that may be used are heating cables (of the type used by horticulturists to warm soil) placed in the substrate; heating pads placed under the terraria; and heat lamps placed outside the terrarium so as to shine through the gauze in the lid (great care should be taken in the use of such lamps to avoid desiccation of the plants and the inmates; temperature can be adjusted by raising or lowering the lamp).

As amphibians are *ectothermic* (body temperature controlled by the surrounding environmental temperature), they maintain their preferred body temperature by moving in or out of warm places. It is therefore advisable to have a range of temperatures available in the terrarium. This can be accomplished by placing the heating apparatus to one end or side. The warmest part will then be near the heater and the temperature will gradually become less as the distance from

Heating pads for under the terrarium are now commonly available.

temperature in the terrarium by 6-8°C (10-12°F) each night. This can be accomplished by simply switching off the heaters in the evening. The prevailing temperature in the average home will be enough to maintain a not too low temperature in the terrarium for the remainder of the

the heater increases. The anurans will then be able to seek out a spot in the terrarium where the temperature suits them best. Where aquarium heaters are used as the sole form of heating the temperature gradient is not so important because, although the water will maintain a reasonably constant temperature, the air temperature will vary by changes in the degree of ventilation.

In most countries there is a lowering of temperature at night, so it is advisable to reduce the

Normal room lighting may not be sufficient for the plants kept in the terrarium or aquarium.

Housing

night. If terraria are kept in unheated rooms where there is a danger of excessively low temperatures in the winter, then some form of supplementary heating must be maintained at night. Another factor that must be taken into consideration is seasonal temperature variation. This is particularly important with temperate species whose breeding cycles are controlled by increases in temperature in the spring.

Lighting: Most frogs and toads are nocturnal and prefer to keep out of the light during the day by burrowing or hiding in nooks and crannies. However, this does not mean that they should be kept in permanent darkness. The photoperiod (length of daylight) is important to many species in their normal daily and breeding cycles. Many temperate species come into breeding condition when influenced by increasing hours of daylight and increasing temperatures in the spring. It is advisable to try and reproduce a light/dark cycle similar to that found in the native habitat of the species in question. If more than one species is kept in the same terrarium, try and choose those that have similar natural photoperiods. It is best to avoid using natural light in indoor terraria as sunlight can soon raise the internal temperature to lethal levels unless great care is taken. However, if plants are to flourish in the terrarium a good quality artificial light will have to be used. Special plant lights are available from pet shops and horticultural suppliers in the form of broad-spectrum fluorescent tubes that emit a quality of light ideal for plant growth. These tubes are available in various sizes and wattages suitable for all kinds of terraria. The lamps can be mounted in special brackets in the aquarium lid, but they must be protected by gauze to prevent the inmates from coming into contact with them.

Ventilation: Good ventilation is essential in the humid environment of the terrarium, but this must be provided without creating excessive drafts. Good ventilation will prevent a buildup of foul air, remove excess carbon dioxide, and prevent the growth of unpleasant molds on the substrate. All lids of terraria must be adequately ventilated; the greater the vented area the better. In fact, a simple frame covered with fine plastic or metal

The spectacular Atelopus varius zeteki is nocturnal and secretive.

mesh is ideal. For even more efficient ventilation, one or more of the sides or parts of the sides of the terrarium can have the glass replaced by acrylic or plexiglass panels into which rows of small holes about 5 mm (1/4 in) in diameter are neatly drilled.

Another method of improving the ventilation in the terrarium is the use of an aquarium aeration pump. These pumps come in various sizes, but a small diaphragm pump will be adequate for a medium terrarium. A plastic tube is run from the pump into the water part of the terrarium. On the end of the tube is an air

help raise the temperature of the air space if the water is heated. Such air pumps are also useful in creating filters and waterfalls.

Humidity: Humidity is essential to most amphibians. We should aim to have a humidity level of 60% or more in the terrarium. The use of an air pump causing air circulation through the water will help keep levels up, but it may still be necessary to spray the interior of the terrarium twice per day,

Small air pumps and corner filters will suffice in many aqua-terrariums.

diffuser stone. When the pump is switched on, tiny bubbles of air will rise to the water surface, creating air movement in the terrarium. Such a system will perform a number of functions. An air pump is essential if tadpoles are being raised as it will aerate the water (by a combination of bubbles and water movement) and increase the oxygen supply. It will help keep the water "sweet." It will create ventilation. It will increase humidity in the air space. It will

especially in areas where the outside atmosphere is dry. This is of particular importance if the terrarium is kept in a room that is centrally heated. Frogs and toads will die very quickly if the humidity is too low. For spraying the plants and other decorations in the terrarium a fine-mist horticultural type spray is recommended.

Filtration: It is highly recommended that a water filter be used in aquaria and aqua-terraria. Many species will quickly

medium must be changed frequently.

For larger volumes of water a power filter is recommended. There are many types available, but the majority consist of large pumps that remove the water from the tank and force it through a filter chamber that may contain layers of various filter media and chemicals that can purify the water. Such filters should be used according to the manufacturer's instructions. By clever use of a filter the returning water can be

Clawed frogs and pipids are large and messy animals that may require a power filter to keep their tank clean.

Outdoor pools and their surrounding vegetation often harbor many frogs.

foul the water, which will not only become evil-smelling but will become unhygienic for the inmates. The simplest type of filter is that known as the box filter. This is operated by the air pump and consists of a (usually) plastic box that is filled with a filter medium such as nylon wool. It works on the principle that rising air bubbles create a current. The air line is placed at the bottom of the tube in the center of the filter. As the air rises it creates a current that continually pulls water through the filter medium, which catches the suspended solids. Such a filter is adequate for a small volume of water, but the filter

Pedostibes hosii *is a small, delicate bufonid that requires a small terrarium.*

made to run back into the tank via a rock wall, thus creating a miniature waterfall, which will also aid humidity levels in the air space. For more details of various filters, it is recommended that the reader refer to a good book on keeping tropical fish.

Greenhouses
Many species of frogs and toads, particularly those from temperate and subtropical areas, are suitable for keeping in conservatories or greenhouses.

In such cases they can be given a free run of the area. If the correct type of breeding pool is available, they should be able to reproduce almost naturally. Even tropical species can be kept in this way, if you can afford to heat your greenhouse to "tropical" temperatures. All windows must of course be covered with gauze (fly-screening is ideal) to prevent the inmates escaping when the windows are opened for ventilation. In a greenhouse it is recommended that large groups of amphibians be kept that should be self-sustaining, providing the correct conditions are given.

Outdoor Housing
Native species can be encouraged to live in your garden by just providing them with a

The very long hind legs of this tropical tree frog, Hyla lanciformis, *mean problems if you try to keep it in a small tank. Good jumpers require both a high tank and great caution whenever the tank lid is opened for even a few seconds.*

pond. Initial stocking is done by adding wild-collected spawn or tadpoles to the pond. Providing conditions are correct and there is adequate plant cover near to the pond, the amphibians will metamorphose and stay in the area, probably breeding in the same pond when reaching maturity. It is usually a waste of time trying to do this if you have fish in the pond, as the fish will eat the tadpoles; you can only have one or the other.

For more confined outdoor accommodations, a wall may be built around a pond and a land area. Ensure that the wall is high enough to keep the frogs from jumping out. It is also wise to have an overhang at the top of the wall to prevent them from climbing over the top. Such an enclosure is one of the best ways to keep and breed native species in controlled conditions. The enclosure can be attractively landscaped with rocks, plants, and perhaps a waterfall, with various ponds at different levels, giving your frogs or toads a choice of breeding sites.

Foods and Feeding

All animals, including frogs and toads, require a balanced diet for their basic metabolism to work correctly. A balanced diet consists of the correct proportions of proteins, carbohydrates, fats, vitamins, and minerals. All frogs are carnivorous in that they eat other animals (in the majority of cases invertebrates) and are fairly non-specific in their diet, consuming a wide range of insects, spiders, worms, and so on. Plant material is not consumed deliberately (except in the tadpole stage of many species), but a certain amount may be taken up in the capture of the prey or from the

most easily available live foods, mealworms for example, that can be readily purchased at regular intervals. Mealworms are an excellent food and most frogs and toads will take them, but there is evidence to suggest that mealworms alone are lacking in certain minerals that are important to metabolism. They should therefore only be given as *part* of a more varied diet.

Collecting Live Foods
Although there are several species of invertebrates that can be purchased at regular intervals or cultured in the home, the collection of a varied supply from

Wild-caught insects, such as this dragonfly, are often acceptable food for your frogs.

undigested contents of the prey animal's gut. In the wild, frogs and toads consume a sufficient variety of organisms to ensure that they have a balanced diet. Temperate species that hibernate in the winter must not only consume enough to give them reserves for hibernation, they must take enough food to see them to the next breeding season. In captivity, it is a great temptation to give anurans the

the wild is highly recommended. Not only will it provide your captives with a greater variety of diet, it will help to relieve boredom to a certain extent (even frogs and toads can get fed up with the same old items on the menu). One of the most productive methods of obtaining a selection of terrestrial insects and spiders is by "sweeping" herbage with a large, sturdy, fine-meshed net (similar to a butterfly

Looking under logs will reveal possible foods for your pets. Slugs, although they may be acceptable to some toads, are best avoided.

net). The net is passed through the foliage of trees, shrubs, and tall grass, and the resulting catch is placed in jars to be transported home. Such a sweep (in the summer months) should provide large numbers of caterpillars, beetles, bugs, grasshoppers, and spiders, all items that frogs and toads will eagerly accept. Do not put too many insects into the terrarium at any one time. Allow the amphibians to eat what is available before adding more, otherwise you will get an overpopulation of insects and

escapees into the house. In addition, the insects will eventually fall into the water, drown, and foul it.

Another good place for collecting invertebrates is under rotten logs and other debris. Woodlice, beetles, and earthworms can be collected in this way. For collecting larger numbers of small insects from flowers, etc., a "pooter" can be used; this is a glass bottle with a cork through which two glass tubes are passed. One of the tubes has a piece of rubber

Foods and Feeding

tubing about 15 cm (6 in) long attached to it. Insects are caught by placing the end of the rubber tube near to them and sucking sharply on the other tube with the mouth. The insects will be pulled through the long tube and fall into the bottle. It is advisable to place a piece of fine mesh over the end of the mouthpiece tube to prevent insects being sucked into the mouth.

A good source of food for very small frogs is aphids, which may often be found on new, green shoots of domestic plants. Sometimes they congregate in large numbers and it is a simple matter to pluck the whole shoot and place it in the terrarium. Moths and other night-flying insects can be captured using a light trap. A white sheet is hung up in a suitable place and a strong light is shone onto it. The insects will be attracted to the sheet and can usually be easily caught and placed into a container.

For aquatic frogs, various small invertebrates can be netted from ponds and streams. Daphnia or water fleas are small crustaceans that are common in stagnant, sunny water with a good algae content. These are ideal for feeding to carnivorous tadpoles and small frogs. Mosquito larvae, bloodworms, and glassworms are all free-swimming insect larvae that can be fed to aquatic species.

By wrapping in cheesecloth a branch or twig infested with aphids, you can have a constant supply of small food for weeks at a time.

Termites are often abundant and make excellent food for many amphibians.

Culturing Live Foods

Although it would be ideal if we could give our charges freshly caught live foods all the year around, this is not always possible. Firstly, we may not have the time to spend each day collecting food. Secondly, colder areas have a distinct shortage of such food in the winter. For staple diets, therefore, we have to rely on cultured live foods that can be obtained from specialist suppliers. Those who do not have the time to culture their own live foods can usually obtain regular supplies from a dealer either directly or by mail order, but it is often more economical and interesting to culture foods yourself once you have the initial stock.

Mealworms:

These are the larvae of the flour beetle, *Tenebrio molitor*. For generations they have been the most convenient and easily obtainable live food for keepers of small carnivores. They can be bought in small or large quantities from dealers, and it is a simple matter

to breed them and maintain a steady stock. Allow a number of the mealworms to pupate and metamorphose into adult beetles. These are brown and about 8 mm (3/8 in) in length. The adult beetles are placed in containers with tight-fitting, ventilated lids along with a 5 cm (2 in) layer of food (a mixture of bran and crushed oats is ideal). A layer of burlap or any open-weave non-synthetic material is placed over

Mealworms are a standard frog and toad food.

Foods and Feeding

the food, and a couple of pieces of carrot or some similar vegetable are placed on top of this to provide the beetles with moisture. The beetles will mate and lay eggs in the bran, and these will hatch and develop into full-sized mealworms in about 16 weeks. By starting a new culture with about 100 adult beetles each month, a regular supply of mealworms of all sizes will be available. The excess adults may also be fed to frogs and toads. The cultures should be kept at 25-30°C (77-86°F) for maximum results.

Living large mealworms are very active and hardy, and they should be fed cautiously to smaller or more delicate frogs.

Some hobbyists insist that mealworms will eat their way out of a small frog. To feel safe you might want to chop up or even boil mealworms fed to delicate species.

Crickets: In recent years, cricket cultures have become readily available. They are a highly nutritious source of food for captive anurans. There are several species available that can be cultured quite easily. An old aquarium tank with a tight-fitting, ventilated lid is ideal for cricket culture. A layer of sawdust is placed in the base and pieces of twisted up newspaper or torn up egg boxes are placed at one end for the crickets to hide in. The crickets may be fed on a mixture of bran and crushed oats as well as occasional pieces of vegetables. A dish containing water-soaked cotton wool will provide the crickets with drinking water. The adults are most likely to lay their eggs in moist sand or vermiculite, so a bowl or two of this should be provided and should be moved to a separate container at regular intervals and replaced by a new one. The eggs will hatch in about 21 days if they are kept at a temperature of 25°C (77°F). The hatchling nymphs are suitable for very small frogs, being about 3 mm (1/8 in) in length. There are four instars (nymphal stages), each one a little larger in body than the former, until reaching the adult size of about 15 mm (5/8 in). Crickets are a versatile live food, being nutritious and available in various sizes.

Large mealworms are probably too hard-bodied to feed to small frogs.

Crickets are easily cultured and are taken at all sizes by many frogs and toads.

Grasshoppers and Locusts: These are also available from specialist suppliers and may also be obtained in various instar sizes up to the adult size of about 5 cm (2 in) in length. The adults are suitable only for very large anurans, but some of the smaller instars are ideal for smaller frogs and toads. Locusts are a little more difficult to breed than crickets. They may be fed on a mixture of bran and crushed oats supplemented by fresh green food that is changed daily. A convenient way of doing this is to place grass stems in a bottle of water and pack wadding around the neck to prevent the insects from falling in and drowning. They are best kept in tall aquaria or ventilated glass-fronted boxes. They lay their eggs in slightly dampened sand to a depth of about 2.5 cm (1 in), so they must be provided with containers in which to do this.

The complete life cycle of common crickets takes about three months. The young may be reared through their instars in the same way that the adults are kept. If a breeding colony of crickets is carefully planned and harvested, it will provide a constant supply of live food throughout the year.

To remove crickets from their container, pick up a piece of the crumpled paper in which they are hiding and shake the required quantity into a jar (being held over the container!). By placing the jar in a refrigerator for ten minutes, the crickets will be slowed down enough to prevent escapes when you are giving them to your animals.

Foods and Feeding

They should be maintained at a temperature of about 28°C (82°F).

Flies: Various species of flies are excellent food for anurans, and there are sizes to suit all. The staple diet of some of the smallest captive frogs has often been fruitflies (*Drosophila*), those little black flies that colonize rotten fruit. A colony can soon be started by placing a box of banana skins or rotten fruit in a corner of the garden. In the summer months this will be teeming with fruitflies in no time at all. The flies may be collected from the area by using a fine-meshed net. Fruitflies are used extensively in laboratories for genetic experiments and are cultured there in jars of agar jelly. Most laboratories that keep them can sometimes be talked into supplying cultures and instructions on their further proliferation. Cultures are also sold by biological supply houses and some mail order food dealers as well as some pet shops.

The lesser housefly, *Fannia canicularis*, and the housefly, *Musca domestica*, are useful foods for small to medium anurans, while the greenbottles,

When they can be collected at the right size, grasshoppers are worth feeding to your pets.

Lucilia species, and bluebottles, *Calliphora* species, are suitable for larger ones. Many flies can be caught during the summer in a fly-trap. This consists basically of a cubical framework (about 30 x 30 x 30 cm, 12 x 12 x 12 in) covered with a fine mesh. This is mounted on a flat board with a 5 cm (2 in) hole in the center over which is placed a transparent funnel. The whole thing is placed in four bricks to raise the board about 5 cm (2 in) from the ground. A piece

Flies of various types, both reared and collected, are nutritious foods.

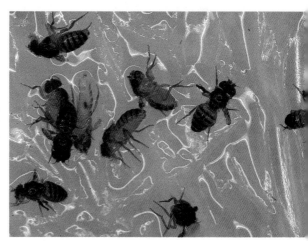

Vestigial-winged fruitflies are excellent for small frogs of all types and are readily cultured.

of evil-smelling bait (rotten fish or meat) is placed under the hole in the board. The flies will be attracted to the bait by smell and will visit it to feed or lay eggs. When disturbed they will make for the nearest source of light: through the hole and up the funnel, where they will be trapped within the mesh framework. The flies can be extracted by having a muslin sleeve on one side of the frame so that a jar can be passed into the container. When not in use the sleeve is knotted at the end.

Another, more convenient, method of obtaining a fly supply is to purchase maggots, which are occasionally available in bait shops. The maggots can be placed in small containers of bran or sawdust, where they will pupate in a few days. In another few days the adult flies will emerge. By having a fly-sized hole in the lid of the container, the flies will escape singly. The whole container may be placed in the terrarium, where the inmates will soon learn the source of food and wait around the hole for the flies.

Although fry maggots (gentles or spikes) are not readily available in the U.S.A., they can sometimes be found in bait shops.

Foods and Feeding

Earthworms: These are a highly nutritious food for many anuran species, although some will refuse to take them. Earthworms come in various sizes depending on their stages of growth and species. A good method of ensuring a fairly continuous supply of earthworms in the summer months is to clear a patch of earth in a corner of the garden, preferably where it is shaded from the sun. Place a 5 cm (2 in) layer of dead leaves over this and peg out a large piece of burlap over the leaves. The sacking is then liberally dampened with water (but not waterlogged) every day. By looking under the sacking and sorting through the leaves at regular intervals, a good supply of earthworms should be forthcoming for several weeks. As the supply diminishes, the collecting area may be moved elsewhere.

Whiteworms: These are slender white worms that grow to about 2 cm (¾ in) in length. Normally found among decaying vegetation, they can be purchased easily as cultures from many pet shops. These are placed in (preferably sterilized) loam in a flat box such as a seed tray. A few pieces of stale brown bread or a few teaspoons of crushed oats are placed in depressions in the surface of the soil. The whole surface is then dampened with a mist spray at daily intervals and covered with a sheet of glass. The culture should be kept in a dark spot at a temperature of around 22°C (72°F). The worms will breed readily and will congregate around the food patches, where they may be teased out with a camelhair brush at regular intervals. They will also readily climb up matchsticks or similar items "planted" in the culture. As such cultures tend to sour or mold very quickly, it is recommended that a new culture be started every two weeks or so until you have four cultures going, each one being discarded at eight weeks of age and replaced by a new one. Worms from the oldest culture can be used to start the next one.

Supplements

Anurans that receive a great variety of invertebrate live foods are not likely to suffer from vitamin or mineral deficiencies. However, occasions arise, particularly during the winter months, when non-hibernating species have to be given cultured live foods such as mealworms or crickets over long periods. In such cases it is highly recommended that a multivitamin and mineral supplement is given

Small crustaceans such as these asellids or water sowbugs can be fed to aquatic frogs.

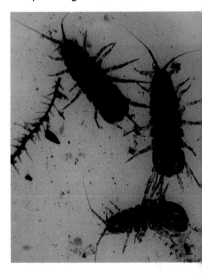

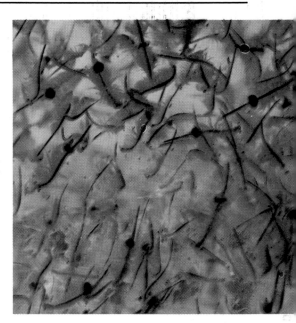

Brine shrimp in both fresh and frozen form are standard fare for clawed frogs.

at regular intervals (say two or three times per week). Multivitamin liquids and powders are available from drug stores, pet shops, and veterinarians. For amphibians, powders are most suitable as they can be dusted directly onto the live food. Place the required number of insects in a container and dust with the powder until a fine film is adhered to the bodies. The insects may then be fed directly to the amphibians.

The proper size insect food is essential for recently transformed froglets.

Feeding Strategies

Most species of anurans can be fed on a daily basis, giving them just the amount of food that they can manage at one time. The correct amounts of food will have to be ascertained by experimentation, but it is better to give too little rather than too much. This is particularly true with aquatic species, where uneaten food will soon foul the water. With terrestrial species it will do no harm if a few food insects are in the cage for a few days, but no further food items should be given until the original ones have been eaten (after ensuring, of course, that what you have given is acceptable as a food item).

Most species of frogs and toads are initially attracted to their prey by its movement, so in the majority of cases it is a waste of time giving dead food. However, some species, particularly the larger toads, can be persuaded to take tiny pieces

Proceratophrys boiei, a tropical horned frog. All horned frogs should be considered cannibalistic.

of lean raw meat by placing it in front of them and jiggling it about with a very fine broom straw. Aquatic species will usually take dead food by smell alone, and these can be given the occasional piece of meat, fish, or shellfish. Such foods, however, do not constitute a balanced diet and should only be used as "fillers" when live food is not available. Some of the largest frogs and toads can be extremely greedy and will eat small vertebrates such as mice, lizards, and each other! In particular, members of the genera *Pyxicephalus* and *Ceratophrys* will have no compunction in eating smaller co-inhabitants of the terrarium, even members of their own species! Caution is therefore advised at all times.

Health and Hygiene

Health and hygiene go hand in hand; without the latter, then the former will suffer. When groups of animals are kept in close confinement, then good practices of hygiene are doubly important. In the dictionary at hand, health is described as: "wholeness or soundness, especially of the body; general state of the body," while hygiene is described as: "the science or art of preserving health." This definition of hygiene may sound as though it can become complicated, but basic hygiene is usually a matter of simple common sense. Many people relate the word "hygiene" to disinfectants, chemicals, and sanitation, but this is only part of it. Providing animals with all they reduces resistance to disease. Many disease organisms are present in the animals themselves and in their air and water at all times. Normally, healthy amphibians will have immune systems in operation that will stop the diseases from taking over the body. In stressed animals the immune systems fail to operate and the animals may come down with diseases they could otherwise fight off.

Selection of Specimens

One of the most important aspects of hygiene is to ensure that one has healthy animals in the first place. When purchasing a specimen from a pet shop, first impressions of the premises can

To be kept healthy, Xenopus *and other aquatic frogs require clean water.*

require to prevent stress is a good hygienic practice in the first place. Frogs and toads are, in general, not very adaptable to surroundings that are alien to them, so sudden changes in temperature, humidity, terrain, and even conditions of acidity or alkalinity can cause stress that

give one a good idea as to the likely state of health of the animals in stock. Dirty, smelly, untidy premises with overstocked terraria are more likely to harbor diseased stock than establishments whose proprietors obviously go out of their way to provide their stock with all necessary requirements and display the animals in a manner designed to impress the customer. Any premises with overcrowded terraria and obvious uncleanliness should be avoided, as there is a high risk that an unpleasant disease may already be present in the stock.

Select specimens that are plump (sunken abdomens and exaggeration of the bones in the pelvic area are sure signs of starvation) and have an unblemished skin (with some of the rough-skinned toads this may take a little practice before you are adept at recognizing skin disorders). The eyes should be open and bright, with correctly

become attached to a frog or toad and admire its beauty or be amazed by its bizarreness, but it is not the kind of animal to be stroked, cuddled, or taken to bed; anyone requiring such a pet should invest in a cat or a dog. No, amphibians are not to be petted; it is bad for them. Their sensitive skins cannot tolerate the salt content of sweaty human hands. Frogs and toads should be handled as little as possible, and only when it is necessary for examination purposes.

*Small frogs such as this chorus frog (*Pseudacris*) are easily damaged if handled roughly.*

shaped pupils. Avoid specimens with dull or cloudy eyes or those that show any sign of inflammation. Specimens should be wary of the hand and should hop or run away when touched. Do not select specimens that show no fight, flight, or fright.

Handling

Amphibians are not animals to be handled and petted at every opportunity and cannot really be described as pets in the strict sense of the word. One can

One such time is when you are purchasing new specimens from a dealer; the hands should be washed under running water to remove excess salt and left wet. The frog or toad then can be gently picked up by cupping one or both hands (depending on the size of the amphibian) over the whole body. The specimen can be examined by opening the fingers, but keeping enough pressure to ensure that it does not leap out. Many frogs have been injured by jumping out of human hands and

Specimens are often damaged during shipping. Even hardy frogs such as this European Rana ridibunda *are easily stressed.*

hitting against hard or sharp objects. With large and powerful specimens such as bullfrogs it is best to stretch out the hind legs and grip the animal gently but firmly around the waist, thus preventing it from bringing its jumping muscles into operation. Aquatic frogs and tadpoles can be caught up in a net and examined without handling at all, apart from moving the net material away from the body.

Remember that many frogs and toads have powerful protective poisons that may be discharged from various glands in the skin, so in addition to washing and wetting the hands before handling for the sake of the animals, it is advisable to wash your hands after handling for your own sake. If certain poisons get into the eyes or mucous membranes they can cause no mean amount of pain and distress! Another thing to be borne in mind, in relation to amphibian poisons, is that some species are unable to tolerate the poisons of others. Great care should be taken in keeping species separate if one is unsure of the result of keeping them together.

Transport
Maximum stress occurs in the transportation of specimens. It is important that we make this potentially traumatic time as easy as possible for our animals. Terrestrial frogs and toads are best placed in plastic boxes with secure lids and containing damp sphagnum moss. The moss serves two purposes—it prevents the animals from becoming desiccated, and it acts as a shock absorber should the container receive rough treatment. Adequate ventilation holes should be drilled in the box. The animals should be transported as quickly as possible to their destination via the shortest possible route. Boxes should not be allowed to

When keeping ranid frogs, beware of possible red leg infections.

chill (especially with regard to tropical species). During the winter in cold climates it is advisable to pack the transport containers inside an insulated styrofoam box. Conversely, transport containers must never be left in the full sun or in a parked car in hot weather, otherwise the animals will soon be literally "cooked."

Quarantine

Whenever new amphibians are acquired with the intention of introducing them to existing stock, perhaps for breeding purposes, it is considered essential that the newcomers undergo a period of quarantine. Many diseases lie dormant in animals, sometimes never causing any problem to the animal unless it becomes stressed. You may have purchased an animal that looks perfectly healthy in every way, but it may be suffering the very early stages of disease brought on by

the trauma of recent capture or transportation. By placing new animals in a special quarantine tank (with all the necessary life support systems but lacking any elaborate decorations) for a minimum of 14 days, you can monitor their health without their being a risk to the health of your existing stock. After the prescribed period of quarantine, the animals can be moved into their permanent homes providing no symptoms of disease have been observed. It is best to keep the quarantine tank in a room separate from existing tanks.

General Hygiene

Ventilation is the key to keeping humid terraria in good condition. Unfortunately, the warm, humid environments required by our tropical frogs and toads also provide ideal conditions for bacteria, fungi, and other undesirable things to multiply. By providing good ventilation in addition to high humidity, growth of certain organisms can be minimized. Garden soil is particularly subject to bacterial growth, and it is best to use only materials that have been pre-sterilized. It is also best to minimize tank decorations to the bare essentials. Tree frogs, for example, can do well on a washed gravel substrate; any plants used can be potted, the pots being hidden behind rocks.

When handling objects in a particular terrarium, always wash the hands thoroughly before going to the next one even if there are no obvious signs of disease. This way you will ensure that you are not the culprit who spreads disease through the stock. Terraria will have to be routinely cleaned out at regular intervals and certainly after an outbreak of disease. In the latter case, all contents of the tank should either be destroyed by burning (plants, branches, etc.) or sterilized (rocks, gravel, water containers) by boiling. Never use commercial disinfectants in a terrarium for amphibians; residual amounts of disinfectant in even the smallest quantities can be stressful and even fatal. The only type of disinfectant recommended for use in cleaning terraria and their contents is a solution of sodium hypochlorite (household bleach). A 10% solution of this chemical

danger from the residue.

Hibernation

Anurans from colder climates hibernate during the winter months either by burying themselves in the mud at the bottom of ponds or by hiding in burrows in the ground deep enough to avoid the frost. During this time the animal's rate of metabolism is reduced to such an extent that it requires barely any oxygen, let alone food. This period of hibernation is important in bringing many species into

When disease hits a terrarium, all the decorations must be changed or sterilized.

will kill off even the most stubborn of bacteria in the terrarium and, provided the container and its contents are adequately rinsed with clean water, there is little

breeding condition. Mating usually occurs after springtime temperatures and photoperiods wake the animals from their winter sleep. Although it is possible to keep such anurans active and feeding all the year around in captivity by keeping the temperatures up, they are unlikely to breed and their lives are likely to be shortened.

Health and Hygiene

A period of simulated hibernation is enough to provide temperate species with all they require for a "normal" life style, including increased prospects of successful breeding. In the fall, reduce the temperature of the terrarium gradually over several days and stop feeding the animals. Remove the terrarium to a frost-free area where the temperature can be maintained at not less than 4°C (39°F) and preferably not more than 10°C (50°F). Alternatively, the animals can be packed in slightly damp sphagnum moss in plastic boxes and kept in the refrigerator at 4-5°C (39-41°F) for two to three months.

Frog and Toad Diseases

Frogs and toads kept in good, hygienic conditions with all their necessary life support systems working properly are remarkably resistant to diseases. Indeed, most outbreaks of disease can usually be traced to some inadequacy in the husbandry. When in doubt about diagnosis or cure, always consult a veterinarian. The following problems may occur from time to time.

Nutritional Deficiencies: As most frogs and toads feed on a variety of invertebrates, nutritional deficiency diseases are only likely to occur where there is lack of variety in the diet (such as when only mealworms are given as food, for example). Various mineral or vitamin deficiencies can cause symptoms such as deformed bone growth, malfunction of the nervous system, skin disorders, and eye troubles. When it is not possible to feed a varied diet for part of the year, it is highly recommended that a suitable vitamin and mineral supplement (preferably in powder form) be added to the staple diet.

Wounds: Open wounds that can become infected with bacteria are usually caused by nervous animals continually jumping against the sides of the terrarium in their efforts to escape. Newly acquired animals should always be left in peace to settle into their new homes and disturbed as little

A marsupial frog shedding and eating its skin. This is normal frog behavior.

48

Tadpoles of all types are very subject to fungal and bacterial infections. This is a Xenopus tadpole.

as possible. Once accustomed to their new surroundings, injury is less likely. For the prevention of bacterial infections in wounds and the promotion of healing, an antibiotic ointment or powder from the drug store or pet shop may be applied, but it is safest to obtain advice from a veterinarian before attempting to use more potent preparations.

Fungal Infections: Fungal infections are particularly common in aquatic amphibians and manifest themselves in areas of inflamed skin surrounded by whitish tissue. Untreated fungal infections can be fatal. The animal should be bathed in a solution of 2% malachite green or Mercurochrome for five minutes. This should be repeated at daily intervals until a cure is effected. If no improvement shows after seven days, a veterinarian should be consulted.

Red Leg: This is a particularly nasty disease of frogs that unfortunately is all too common. It may be caused by a variety of bacteria and can be fatal unless treated. Symptoms include red areas on the thighs, but this should not be confused with the many frog species that have natural red coloration in this area. Immersion in a 2% solution of copper sulphate solution may cure the affliction. The use of antibiotics may be helpful. It is recommended that a veterinarian be consulted for the best course to take. The disease is highly contagious and has been known to destroy all the specimens being kept in a breeding facility.

The first few days out of the water are a difficult time for most froglets, and many die.

Popular and Interesting Species

With over 4000 species of frogs and toads known to science, it would be impossible to list more than a few in a volume of this size. Therefore, the author has attempted to assemble a list of better known species from various genera, most of which will breed in captivity given the right conditions. In addition, a few more "difficult" species have been added to whet the appetite of those who, having gained experience with the commoner types, wish to advance to more ambitious projects.

Frogs and toads may be purchased from dealers who specialize in reptiles and amphibians and from enthusiasts already in the process of regular captive breeding of certain species. You also may be able to collect specimens from the wild, but before taking this latter course it is advisable to make yourself aware of national and local laws regarding the protection of wildlife. While most frogs are not protected, some species may be protected in local areas (such as national parks or states in which they are uncommon) and a few may be totally protected in certain countries. It can be a serious offense to take protected species from the wild or even to possess them, so beware!

In the following list, the lengths given are the normal maximum size you may expect of an adult; in most cases specimens are likely to mature at somewhat smaller sizes.

African Clawed Frog
Xenopus laevis
Family Pipidae
Length: 12.5 cm (5 in)
DESCRIPTION: The clawed frog has a smooth, slippery skin and powerful hind legs well adapted for swimming. The dorsal surface is gray to brown, marbled with darker shades; the underside is creamy white. The name *Xenopus*, literally "strange foot," is derived from the sharp "claws" on the toes of the hind feet. Albinos are available.
NATURAL RANGE: Southern Africa, but introduced to many parts of

The African clawed frog, Xenopus laevis.

the world. Now prohibited in many western areas of the U.S.A. because it has become a dangerous pest.

HABITAT AND HABITS: Found in a variety of slow-moving waters, usually in muddy or well-planted areas. Finds its prey by smell and touch.

CAPTIVE CARE: Provide a large aquarium containing water about 30 cm (12 in) deep for these aquatic frogs. A gravel substrate and a filter are necessary.

was found that if the urine of pregnant women was injected into a pair of the toads, the hormones present would cause immediate mating to occur, with the laying of fertile eggs just a couple of days later. This fact is used by commercial producers of *Xenopus* frogs, and special hormone kits are available to induce the amphibians to breed. The small eggs usually fall to the bottom of the tank, where they can be removed with a pipette

The typical circular spawning behavior of clawed frogs.

Temperature about 24°C (75°F). Floating plants and rocks may be added for decoration but are not strictly necessary. Will take small pieces of lean raw meat and fish as well as the usual invertebrates.

BREEDING: *Xenopus* is famous for its use in the pioneering methods of pregnancy testing in humans. It

and placed in a separate container of aerated water. The tadpoles, which are remarkably fish-like in appearance, may be fed on a suspension of dried green pea soup or powdered grass (in small quantities). The young toads will metamorphose in six to eight weeks given the

A dwarf clawed frog, Hymenochirus.

right conditions. As soon as the legs appear, they will start taking small aquatic invertebrates.

RELATED SPECIES: *X. muelleri* and *X. borealis* are slightly smaller species with similar habits and requiring similar husbandry.

Dwarf Clawed Frog
Hymenochirus boettgeri
Family Pipidae
Length 3.5 cm (1½ in)
DESCRIPTION: This very small anuran bears a superficial resemblance to the Surinam toad, to which it is distantly related. It is grayish or brownish, with darker marbling; paler on the underside. The skin texture is much rougher than in a small *Xenopus*.
NATURAL RANGE: Central and western Africa.
HABITAT AND HABITS: Totally aquatic; found in still and slow-moving waters.
CAPTIVE CARE: Similar to that described for *Xenopus*, but shallower water. Food items must be relatively smaller.
BREEDING: Raising the temperature of the water from 24° to 27°C (75° to 81°F) will stimulate breeding behavior. The male grasps the female in front of the hind legs and they rise to the surface and turn over on their backs. The male pumps the female and 10-20 tiny eggs are laid. The pair then sink. The process is repeated until as many as 1000 eggs have been laid. These sink to the bottom of the tank and may be removed with a pipette for hatching in a separate container of clean, aerated water. The tadpoles hatch in two to three days, and in another three days they will be feeding upon microorganisms.

Surinam Toad
Pipa pipa
Family Pipidae
Length: 20 cm (8 in)
DESCRIPTION: This is a really

Hymenochirus tadpoles.

bizarre species with a flattened body and pointed snout. The front legs are small. The fingers end in star-like appendages that are extremely sensitive to touch and are used to locate food items in murky waters. The hind legs are large and powerful, ending in huge webbed feet. The eyes are very small, inconspicuous, and on the top of the head (as in other pipid frogs). The body color is a mixture of browns and grays on the rough skin of the back, but lighter beneath.

NATURAL RANGE: Northern rain forest regions of South America.

HABITAT AND HABITS: Found in slow-moving rivers or streams, often among dead vegetation, where it is remarkably camouflaged.

CAPTIVE CARE: An adult pair may be kept in a large aquarium with a water depth of about 30 cm (12 in) and a temperature of 27°C (81°F). Robust aquatic plants should be used as the toads can be quite violent with their surroundings. They will feed on small live fishes as well as earthworms, strips of meat, and dead fish, which they usually find by touch. An aquarium filter is considered essential for these animals.

BREEDING: In keeping with the bizarre appearance, the breeding habits of this species are most unusual. They can be brought into breeding condition by reducing the temperature to about 22°C (72°F) and raising the water level. The male grasps the female in front of the hind legs, and a series of somersaults are performed. While in the upside-down position, the female releases a

Pipa carvalhoi *giving "birth" to its tadpoles. Some* Pipa *give birth to froglets.*

number of small eggs that are immediately pushed into the porous skin of her back by the male as he fertilizes them. Some eggs also will fall to the substrate, but these will not develop and are best removed with a pipette and

disposed of once mating activities are complete. After performing several somersaults and laying 60-80 eggs, the pair will separate. In 24 hours or so the skin of the female's back will begin to swell around the eggs, this process continuing until each egg is embedded in its own individual chamber. Complete development and metamorphosis of the larvae occur in these chambers. Perfectly formed little Surinam toads will emerge from the female's back in 12-20 weeks. These should be removed and reared in a separate tank on tiny aquatic invertebrates.

Common Eurasian Spadefoot
Pelobates fuscus
Family Pelobatidae
Length: 8 cm (3¼ in)
DESCRIPTION: Members of the family Pelobatidae are

The circular spawning behavior of Pipa *closely resembles that of other clawed frogs.*

distinguished in having a prominent, flattened, sharp-edged "spade" on the heel of the foot. The common Eurasian spadefoot is a plump, toad-like anuran with prominent eyes and vertical pupils. The body color is buff marked with blotches or stripes of light brown. The underside is whitish.
NATURAL RANGE: Lowland western, central, and eastern Europe into western Asia.
HABITAT AND HABITS: Spadefoots are normally confined to areas with sandy soil. Outside the breeding season they are nocturnal, hiding in burrows that they excavate with the spade-like tubercles on their hind feet.

CAPTIVE CARE: They should be kept in a spacious terrarium with a sandy substrate at least 10 cm (4 in) deep into which they will burrow and hide during the day. A large dish of water should be provided and the substrate should be sprayed regularly to maintain humidity (but *no* waterlogging). Food consists of various small invertebrates. It is recommended that this species be hibernated at 3-4°C (37-39°F) for three months. Normal daytime temperatures are 18-22°C (65-72°F), reduced to 15°C (59°F) at night.

BREEDING: It is unlikely that this species will breed in the confines of an indoor terrarium. An outdoor enclosure with sandy areas and a deep (90 cm, 3 ft) pond is required for successful breeding. The eggs are laid in thick bands usually wound around the stems of waterplants. The tadpoles are exceptionally large compared to the size of the adults

Couch's spadefoot toad, Scaphiopus couchi.

and may reach 17.5 cm (7 in) in length.

RELATED SPECIES: The western Eurasian spadefoot, *P. cultripes*, from southwestern France and Spain, and the eastern Eurasian spadefoot, *P. syriacus*, from the Balkans and Asia Minor, are similar in habits and require similar husbandry though slightly warmer summer temperatures and a shorter period of hibernation, two months at 5°C (41°F).

Plains Spadefoot Toad
Scaphiopus bombifrons
Family Pelobatidae
Length: 6 cm (2½ in)
DESCRIPTION: The five species in the North American genus *Scaphiopus* are the equivalent of the Eurasian *Pelobates*. The plains spadefoot toad is a plump little amphibian with relatively large eyes. The body color is a mixture of buff and bronze arranged into vague stripes or blotches, often with overtones of green. Scattered tubercles on the skin may be reddish brown to orange.

NATURAL RANGE: The Great Plains

from Canada to Texas and northern Mexico.

HABITAT AND HABITS: Lives in shortgrass prairie where the soil is loose and dry, inhabiting burrows up to 90 cm (3 ft) in length. Emerges at night to hunt invertebrates.

CAPTIVE CARE: A medium sized terrarium with a deep (15 cm, 6 in) sandy substrate. A dish of water should be available, but the substrate may be kept reasonably dry. Daytime temperatures to 27°C (81°F), but reduced to 15°C (59°F) at night. Feed on a variety of small invertebrates. Hibernate two to three months at 3-4°C (37-39°F).

spadefoot toad, *S. hammondi*, and the eastern spadefoot toad, *S. holbrooki* (not to be confused with the eastern and western Eurasian spadefoots). All require similar husbandry.

Asian Horned Frog
Megophrys nasuta
Family Pelobatidae
Length: 12.5 cm (5 in)
DESCRIPTION: This is a bizarre species with a fleshy horn above each eye and another at the end of the snout. The color is a mixture of browns and reddish browns that provides good camouflage in its habitat.
NATURAL RANGE: Southeast Asia.

Scaphiopus hammondi, *another common spadefoot toad from the western United States.*

BREEDING: Captive-breeding in the indoor terrarium is unknown. In the wild the species breeds after heavy rains and flash floods. The tadpoles have rapid growth and metamorphose in two months. Breeding results may be successful in outdoor enclosures in appropriate climates.

RELATED SPECIES: There are four other North American species in the genus, including the western

HABITAT AND HABITS: Usually found on the ground among leaf litter in thickly wooded areas. Partially burrows itself into the substrate, from whence it will lunge at passing food items at any time of the day or night.

CAPTIVE CARE: A tropical aqua-terrarium with about one-third water and two-thirds land. The land area should have a good depth of leaf litter in which the

The Asian horned frog, Megophrys nasuta.

frogs will hide. Tropical plants and a high humidity are recommended. Food can consist of larger invertebrates such as mealworms, locusts, etc. Average temperature is 26°C (79°F), reduced slightly at night. Temperatures may remain fairly constant all year. No hibernation is required.

BREEDING: Seldom bred in captivity. Females are much larger than males. The eggs are attached to the roof of a cave or a leaf just above the water level, the tadpoles emerging after 11 days and sliding into the water. Tadpoles feed on finely pulverized food at the surface. Metamorphosis at about 2½ months.

Midwife Toad

Alytes obstetricans
Family Discoglossidae
Length: 5 cm (2 in)
DESCRIPTION: Members of the family Discoglossidae are characterized by having a tongue that cannot be extended as in most other anuran families. Food is simply grabbed in the mouth and often pushed into the gullet with the forelimbs. The midwife toad is a small, plump anuran with large eyes and vertical pupils. Color is usually gray, olive, or brown with darker markings.
NATURAL RANGE: Western Europe from central Germany south into the Iberian peninsula.
HABITAT AND HABITS: Frequents woodlands, gardens, quarries, and rocky screes up to an altitude of 2000 m (6500 ft.) Mainly nocturnal. Calls at night with a

Popular and Interesting Species

bell-like tone. During the day it hides in crevices, under logs or rocks, or in self-excavated burrows.

CAPTIVE CARE: Requires a large, terrestrial terrarium with a small water container. Plenty of cover should be provided in the way of flat stones, hollow logs, or broken flowerpots. Temperature about 25°C (77°F), reduced to 18°C (65°F) at night. Hibernate for two to three months at 5°C (41°F).

BREEDING: Breeding is unlikely in the home terrarium but may be possible in an outdoor enclosure. Mating and oviposition take place entirely out of water. The male attracts a female by calling, then clasps her high up on the back. She lays 20-40 eggs in a string. The male winds the string of eggs around his hind legs and carries them around for protection, keeping them moist by occasionally entering shallow pools and puddles. When the eggs are ready to hatch he deposits them in small pools. The tadpoles grow to a large size and the newly metamorphosed toads are relatively large.

Yellow-bellied Toad

Bombina variegata
Family Discoglossidae
Length: 5 cm (2 in)
DESCRIPTION: These little toads are extremely attractive. The warty body is gray-brown on the dorsal surface but bright yellow with dark markings beneath.

NATURAL RANGE: Most of central and southern Europe except Iberia and the Mediterranean islands.

HABITAT AND HABITS: This anuran is largely diurnal, though it may be

Bombina variegata is perhaps the least colorful bombinid.

Views of the bellies of Bombina orientalis *(top) and* Bombina bombina *(bottom). The origin of the common name "fire-bellied toad" for these species should be obvious.*

active at night. It spends much of its time in water, floating on the surface and catching floating insects. Found in a variety of waters, including ponds, marshes, edges of rivers and streams, ditches, and even cart ruts.

CAPTIVE CARE: A large aqua-terrarium is needed for a group of these little toads, with rather more water than land (one-third land to two-thirds water). The water should be about 15 cm (6 in) deep, filtered and aerated, and with aquatic plants used for decoration. Provide a temperature of about 25°C (77°F), reduced slightly at night. Hibernate for about three months at 3-4°C (37-39°F).

BREEDING: This species frequently has been bred in captivity, both in indoor terraria and outdoor enclosures. Eggs are laid in clumps of about 100. They should be removed to a separate container for hatching and rearing, preferably in pond water that is aerated. The tadpoles will feed on algae or suspended vegetable matter.

Popular and Interesting Species

RELATED SPECIES: The fire-bellied toad, *Bombina bombina*, is a closely related species from eastern Europe. It is very similar in appearance except that the belly is fiery red. The Oriental fire-bellied toad, *Bombina orientalis*, from Siberia, China, and Korea, is somewhat larger (7 cm, 2¾ in)

A European common frog, Rana temporaria.

and has black and green marbling on the back as well as a fiery red belly. All species require similar husbandry, except that the Oriental does not require hibernation and can be kept at slightly higher temperatures.

Painted Frog
Discoglossus pictus
Family Discoglossidae
Length: 7 cm (2¾ in)

DESCRIPTION: Although related to the fire-bellied toads, this species is more superficially frog-like in appearance, with a smooth, slippery skin and long hind legs. It is very variable in color and may be gray, brown, yellowish, or even reddish above, with darker, often light-edged, spots. There may be a light stripe down the back. The underside is whitish, usually with darker speckling.

NATURAL RANGE: Southern France, Iberian Peninsula, Sicily, Malta, and North Africa.

HABITAT AND HABITS: May be active by day or by night and is usually found in or around still or running water, including streams, ponds, cisterns, and ditches.

CAPTIVE CARE: A large aqua-terrarium with two-thirds water (about 15 cm, 6 in deep) and one-third land. Provide aquatic plants and hiding places on the land area. Temperature about 25°C (77°F), reduced somewhat at night. Hibernate for two months at around 5-6°C (41-43°F).

BREEDING: Most easily accomplished in an outdoor pond. About 1000 eggs are scattered among aquatic plants or on the substrate. Newly metamorphosed froglets require tiny invertebrate food.

European Common Frog
Rana temporaria
Family Ranidae
Length: 10 cm (4 in)
DESCRIPTION: The family Ranidae contains a great number of species found in every continent except Antarctica. They can be regarded as "typical frogs," with smooth skin and long, powerful hind legs. The European common frog is highly variable in color and may range through shades of gray, brown, olive, reddish, or yellowish above, with darker

blotches. There is usually a black patch from the rear of the eye to the corner of the mouth. The underside is mainly yellowish white with darker marbling.

NATURAL RANGE: The whole of central and northern Europe as far north as the Arctic Circle. Absent from most of southern Europe.

HABITAT AND HABITS: A mainly terrestrial species that frequents water only in the breeding season. Found in grassy meadows, woodland, and gardens, usually not far from permanent water. May be active during the day or at night.

CAPTIVE CARE: Mainly suited for outdoor ponds or enclosures. Should be kept at temperatures no higher than 20°C (68°F), reduced at night. Requires high humidity.

BREEDING: Breeds well in outdoor ponds. The breeding behavior is that of a "typical" frog.

RELATED SPECIES: Closely related "brown frogs" in Europe include the moor frog, *Rana arvalis*; agile frog, *Rana dalmatina*; stream frog, *Rana graeca*; and Iberian frog, *Rana iberica*. All require similar husbandry, but southern species require higher temperatures.

Edible Frog
Rana esculenta
Family Ranidae
Length: 12 cm (4¾ in)

DESCRIPTION: A robust "green" frog but may be predominantly green or brown, with darker markings. Frequently there is a light-colored stripe down the spine. The males have whitish paired vocal sacs with which they can croak very loudly.

NATURAL RANGE: Through central Europe and Italy. Absent from Iberia and the Balkans.

HABITAT AND HABITS: Found frequently in fairly deep, still waters. Often sunbathes on the bank and leaps into the water at

*The European pond frogs (*Rana esculenta *and allies) are hard to identify.*

the slightest disturbance. May catch food in or out of water.
CAPTIVE CARE: Requires a large aqua-terrarium with a water area at least 30 cm (12 in) deep. Perhaps better suited to an outdoor enclosure with a deep pond. Feeds on a variety of invertebrates. Summer temperatures around 25°C (77°F), reduced at night. Hibernate for about three months at 4-5°C (39-41°F).
BREEDING: Usually bred in outdoor ponds, where up to 10,000 eggs

ranges overlap considerably, which often causes confusion. Many herpetologists believe that the edible frog is actually a fertile hybrid of the other two species.

Bullfrog
Rana catesbeiana
Family Ranidae
Length: 20 cm (8 in)
DESCRIPTION: This is a very large and robust frog species. Usually green to olive green above, mottled with gray or brown. The powerful hind legs are usually

per female are laid. Unlikely to breed in small indoor terraria.
RELATED SPECIES: The larger (15 cm, 6 in) marsh frog, *Rana ridibunda*, and the smaller (9 cm, 3½ in) pool frog, *Rana lessonae*, are similar apart from size and require similar husbandry. All three species are found in Europe, and in some areas their

*Because of their size, bullfrogs (*Rana catesbeiana*) are not suitable for the average terrarium.*

banded in dark and light brown. The eardrums are very prominent, especially in males. It has a single vocal sac beneath the chin. The deep, groaning call is said to

resemble the bellowing of a bull.
NATURAL RANGE: Central and eastern U.S.A. Introduced to the West Coast and to many other parts of the world.
HABITAT AND HABITS: A very aquatic species found in lakes, marshes, deep ponds, and small rivers. Prefers highly vegetated waters. Active by day and night but usually calls at night.
CAPTIVE CARE: Requires a very large aqua-terrarium or preferably a greenhouse or outdoor enclosure with a deep (at least 60 cm, 24 in) pool. A temperature of 20-26°C (68-79°F) is required in the summer, with slight reduction at night. Hibernate in winter for two to three months at 4-5°C (39-41°F). Feeds on larger invertebrates or small vertebrates. Has a huge appetite and must be fed regularly. May be cannibalistic.
BREEDING: Breeding is unlikely unless a very large and deep, vegetated pool is available, either in a greenhouse or outdoors. Tadpoles grow very large and may pass the winter in the larval stage. Commercially bred as a food animal.

Northern Leopard Frog
Rana pipiens
Family Ranidae
Length: 8 cm (3¼ in)
DESCRIPTION: This is a slender brownish to greenish frog with large dark spots in two rows, usually edged with gray or white. It has a light stripe along the upper jaw.
NATURAL RANGE: Southeastern Canada and northern half of the U.S.A. Leopard frogs formerly assigned to *R. pipiens* but from other parts of the U.S.A. and Canada are now distinguished as some six to ten distinct species. All leopard frogs can be treated alike, however.
HABITAT AND HABITS: Found in a variety of sites from freshwater lakes with thick vegetation to brackish marshland. Primarily nocturnal, it takes cover in the water when threatened.
CAPTIVE CARE: A large aqua-terrarium with half land and half water, the water to a depth of 15 cm (6 in). Aquatic and terrestrial plants may be used. A maximum temperature of 25°C (77°F), reduced to about 15°C (59°F) at night. Feed on various small

*The American leopard frogs (*Rana pipiens *and allies) form a very difficult to identify group of frogs found over much of the U.S.A. and Mexico.*

invertebrates. Hibernate for about three months at 3-4°C (37-39°F).
BREEDING: Breeding is most likely to occur in outdoor enclosures with sizable pools. Heavily cultured as a laboratory animal.
RELATED SPECIES: There are several other species of ranids in North America that require similar care including: crawfish frog, *Rana areolata*; green frog, *Rana clamitans*; pig frog, *Rana grylio*; river frog, *Rana heckscheri*; southern leopard frog, *Rana sphenocephala*; mink frog, *Rana septentrionalis*; wood frog, *Rana sylvatica*; and carpenter frog, *Rana virgatipes*. *R. grylio, heckscheri, septentrionalis*, and *virgatipes* are actually much more aquatic than the leopard frogs.

African Bullfrog
Pyxicephalus adspersus
Family Ranidae
Length: 20 cm (8 in)
DESCRIPTION: This frog is a favorite with terrarium keepers, probably due to its enormous size and somewhat grotesque appearance. It is mainly green on the upper surface, which is ornamented by a number of raised longitudinal ridges. The underside is a creamy

Rana pipiens is the common leopard frog of the northeastern U.S.A. and is raised commercially.

yellow, becoming bright yellow to orange on the throat and under the forelimbs. There are large canine-like projections on the lower jaw. Large adults can give vicious bites.
NATURAL RANGE: Southern Africa.
HABITAT AND HABITS: Lives in fairly arid areas, where it estivates during very dry periods. Intense mating activity takes place after heavy rains when surface water is available. This is an extremely voracious species, and larger specimens will eat the smaller ones. It has been suggested that specimens do not reach full adult size until the age of 28 years!
CAPTIVE CARE: In spite of its large size, this species will make do with a fairly small terrarium. It will spend most of its time partially buried in the substrate (a mixture of gravel and leaf litter), ready to lunge at any food item offered to it. It will take a variety of large invertebrates, including earthworms, locusts, cockroaches, and beetles. Adult

specimens are quite capable of dispatching a fully grown mouse! Care should be taken not to overfeed, as obesity can lead to premature death. On no account should it be kept with smaller anurans, even of its own species. It should be provided with a water vessel in which it will regularly bathe. Keep it at an average temperature of 28°C (82°F), which may be reduced by a few degrees at night.

BREEDING: This species is only likely to breed if kept in a heated greenhouse where a large body of water can be provided. After spawning in the normal ranid way, adult males stay in the water near the eggs. They will aggressively defend the eggs and later the large swarm of tadpoles.

Green Poison Arrow Frog
Dendrobates auratus
Family Dendrobatidae
Length: 3.5 cm (1½ in)
DESCRIPTION: Dendrobatids (poison arrow or poison dart frogs) are sometimes classed as a subfamily of Ranidae, but here we follow current use in giving them their own family status. Dendrobatidae is a family of very small, usually highly colored frogs that make interesting inmates for

The African bullfrog, Pyxicephalus adspersus, *is one of the largest frogs and one of the very few that can inflict a serious bite. (Horned frogs are the others.)*

the tropical terrarium. The often bright colors warn predators of the poisonous properties of the frogs that have been exploited by South American Indians. The body fluids are extracted by heating the frogs over a fire and used to tip the points of hunting arrows.

Popular and Interesting Species

The green poison arrow frog is one of the species most commonly seen in captivity. It is enamel black with metallic green stripes usually extending across the body, but much variation occurs, including spots or stripes in the other direction (nose to tail).

NATURAL RANGE: Nicaragua and Costa Rica south to Colombia.

HABITAT AND HABITS: Dendrobatids are inhabitants of the tropical rain forests and are particularly at home among the bromeliads, ferns, and other epiphytes of the tree canopy. They are diurnal and protected from predators by their warning coloration.

CAPTIVE CARE: Poison arrow frogs are not difficult to maintain, providing a steady supply of small invertebrates is available for feeding. During the summer foliage sweepings should be collected on a regular basis, while in winter hatchling crickets and fruitfly cultures are a necessity. Some are also fond of small non-stinging ants. A tall planted terrarium should be prepared, preferably with bromeliads or other water-holding plants. High humidity is essential, and it is advisable to have running or dripping water controlled by an airlift or power filter. Failing this, the terrarium should be misted with a fine spray at least twice per day. Deep water should be avoided as the frogs are poor swimmers and likely to drown. A shallow water dish should contain plenty of stones or pebbles in it to allow easy access and egress. A temperature of 25-28°C (77-82°F) should be maintained throughout the year, but this may be reduced

Green poison arrow frogs, Dendrobates auratus, *are relatively hardy under the right conditions.*

Common poison arrow frogs. Above: Dendrobates lehmanni. Below left: Dendrobates pumilio. Below right: Dendrobates histrionicus. *Although delicate, poison arrow frogs are now being raised commercially.*

Popular and Interesting Species

to around 20°C (68°F) at night.
BREEDING: Breeding has been
accomplished with several
species. When in breeding
condition, the male will select a
spot on a branch or leaf and call
incessantly. Sometimes another
male will try to take over the
territory and a minor wrestling

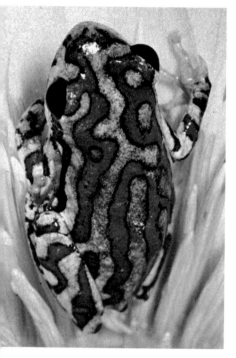

A brightly colored African reed frog,
Hyperolius *species.*

match will develop. Such fights
rarely result in injury, and the
strongest male will keep his
position. Eventually a female will
approach the dominant male and
they will together seek out a
suitable spawning site, usually the
surface of a leaf. A small clump of
eggs is deposited by the female
and these are fertilized by the
male. The male frog waits near
the eggs until they hatch, then
maneuvers the tadpoles onto his

back and transports them to
water, where they are released
and continue normal
development. The tadpoles often
develop in the water-filled bracts
of bromeliads. If these plants are
maintained in the terrarium,
almost natural breeding will take
place.

RELATED SPECIES: There are three
genera of dendrobatids, all with
similar life histories. Some of the
more commonly available species
include the strawberry poison
arrow frog, *Dendrobates pumilio*;
the red and black poison arrow
frog, *Dendrobates histrionicus*;
the yellow-banded poison arrow
frog, *Dendrobates leucomelas*;
and the ornate poison arrow frog,
Phyllobates lugubris.

Reed Frogs

Hyperolius species
Family Rhacophoridae
Length: Up to 4 cm (1½ in)
DESCRIPTION: Reed frogs are all of
similar size and appearance.
Most have adhesive pads on their
toes for climbing. There are many
species and a tremendous
variation in color even in a single
species, but most are various
shades of green and yellow, often
with red and black.
NATURAL RANGE: Many parts of
Africa south of the Sahara.
HABITAT AND HABITS: As the
common name implies, reed frogs
are found in marshy areas among
tall grasses and reeds. They are
active both during the day and at
night.
CAPTIVE CARE: A tall aqua-
terrarium is required, with sturdy
grasses or reed-like plants. A high
humidity and temperatures of 22-
28°C (72-82°F) are recommended.
They should be fed on a variety of
small invertebrates.
BREEDING: Several species have

been bred in captivity. Small clumps of eggs are laid in the water. These should be carefully removed and placed in a separate container of aerated water for hatching and development.

Running Frog

Kassina senegalensis
Family Rhacophoridae
Length: 4 cm (1½ in)
DESCRIPTION: An attractive little frog that is frequently kept in the terrarium, the running frog is marked with light brown and black stripes. It is largely

water dish should be supplied. High humidity and a temperature of around 26°C (79°F) are recommended. Food consists of a variety of small invertebrates. BREEDING: This species lays its eggs directly into water. For breeding, a large aqua-terrarium with moving water (produced by an airlift) is recommended.

African Gray or Foam Nest Tree Frog

Chiromantis xerampelina
Family Rhacophoridae
Length: 6 cm (2½ in)

Hyperolius horstockii, *a more sedately colored reed frog.*

terrestrial and without toe pads.
NATURAL RANGE: Western Africa.
HABITAT AND HABITS: As its common name implies, this species runs rapidly across the substrate rather than hops but it is capable of hopping should the occasion arise. This is one of the few frogs with a visible neck. They are mainly crepuscular and nocturnal.
CAPTIVE CARE: A small terrarium with a large land area, preferably with a substrate covered with moss and a few tropical plants. A

DESCRIPTION: This charming little frog is attractively marked in various shades of gray. It has prominent adhesive toe pads.
NATURAL RANGE: Tropical Africa.
HABITAT AND HABITS: Mainly nocturnal, this species spends the day hiding in crevices in the bark of trees, where its coloration provides excellent camouflage.
CAPTIVE CARE: A tall aqua-terrarium is required, with "barky" branches and a few climbing plants. A daytime temperature of around 26°C (79°F) is

Popular and Interesting Species

recommended, reduced by a few degrees at night. Food consists of a variety of small invertebrates. BREEDING: This and a number of other species in the family construct foam nests. A leafy bough overhanging the water is selected and the spawn is laid on the leaves in a frothy mass that is produced by beating a quantity of specially produced fluid with the hind legs. This foam nest protects the eggs against desiccation until they hatch, when the tadpoles

Malaysian Narrow-mouthed Toad
Kaloula pulchra
Family Microhylidae
Length: 8 cm (3¼ in)
DESCRIPTION: The family Microhylidae is usually known as the narrow-mouthed toads due to the relatively small gape and the pointed snout. *Kaloula pulchra* is frequently available on the market and is a popular terrarium species. It is somewhat squat and toad-like in shape. The ground

The running frog, Kassina senegalensis, is one of the few frogs with a distinct neck region.

wriggle out of the nest and drop into the water, after which they develop in the usual manner. For captive breeding it is essential to provide plants that overhang the water container. High humidity and regular spraying are required to encourage the frogs to breed.

color is usually chestnut brown, lighter on the underside. The distinguishing feature is the broad dark-edged irregular band of cream or reddish buff that extends from each eye down either side of the back to the hind legs.

The foam nest tree frogs of Africa share their breeding habits with some American tree frogs. *Chiromantis xerampelina.*

The Malaysian narrow-mouthed toad, Kaloula pulchra, *is often available to hobbyists.*

NATURAL RANGE: Southeast Asia.
HABITAT AND HABITS: A nocturnal species that estivates in dry periods and is brought into action by heavy rains. In its native

habitat it is often found near human habitations, where it may hunt insects under street lamps and porch lights.

CAPTIVE CARE: One of the easiest of tropical frogs to keep. Requires a terrarium with a deep substrate (5 cm, 2 in) of leaf litter into which it will burrow during the day, coming out at night to feed. Will tolerate temperatures as high as 30°C (86°F), but requires high humidity for it to remain active.

BREEDING: Breeds in marshy pools after heavy rains. The male has a loud "mooing" call to attract the females. Breeding success in captivity is most likely in a tropical greenhouse with a large water

of the back. There are two prominent digging "spades" on each hind foot.

NATURAL RANGE: South Texas and adjacent Mexico to Costa Rica.

HABITAT AND HABITS: Found mainly in moist places in arid areas. Mainly nocturnal, hiding under logs, in termite nests, or in the burrows of rodents during the day. Heavy rain causes it to become active.

CAPTIVE CARE: Requires a terrarium with a sandy substrate and a low humidity, but a shallow water dish should be provided so that the amphibians can seek out moisture if they so wish. Adequate hiding places in the

Toads are often difficult to identify. This Bufo boreas *from the western U.S.A. looks much like* Bufo bufo.

area. Simulated heavy rainfall might bring the frogs into breeding condition.

Sheep Frog

Hypopachus variolosus
Family Microhylidae
Length: 4.5 cm (1¾ in)

DESCRIPTION: This little frog is noted for its loud call that resembles the bleating of a sheep. It is small and plump, with smooth skin and a pointed snout. The color is olive to brown, with a light yellow line down the middle

form of flat pieces of bark should be provided. Temperature 28°C (82°F), reduced at night. The food is mainly ants.

BREEDING: Reproductive behavior may be initiated by spraying of the substrate with lukewarm water. Eggs are laid in the water and hatch within 24 hours. Tadpoles metamorphose into froglets in four weeks or less.

RELATED SPECIES: The eastern narrow-mouthed frog, *Gastrophryne carolinensis*, and the Great Plains narrow-mouthed

Bufo bufo is the common European toad and the "hop toad" of children's literature.

frog, *Gastrophryne olivacea*, both from North America, require similar husbandry.

Common European Toad
Bufo bufo
Family Bufonidae
Length: 15 cm (6 in)
DESCRIPTION: This is the typical European toad and was the first in the genus to be described by Linnaeus. The dry, warty skin is usually brown above, but may be yellowish or reddish depending on the habitat. Often takes on a color resembling the earth in which it lives. The underside is off-white, usually with dark gray marbling.
NATURAL RANGE: Almost the whole of Europe and across central Asia as far as Japan.

HABITAT AND HABITS: Found in a wide variety of fairly dry habitats. Usually nocturnal. It hides by day under logs, stones, and other ground litter. It normally walks, but will hop when alarmed.
CAPTIVE CARE: Provide an unheated, fairly dry terrarium with a substrate of peat, sand, and leaf litter. A couple of hollow logs or broken crocks should be provided to give a choice of hiding places. The temperature should not exceed 22°C (72°F), and this can be reduced to 12°C (54°F) at night. A small water dish is adequate for a terrarium containing a group of non-breeding toads. Food consists of a variety of small invertebrates. The toads should be hibernated in the winter at a temperature of 4-5°C (39-41°F).
BREEDING: This species breeds in the early spring. The males first assemble at suitable ponds, the females arriving several days

later. Males often outnumber females by as many as 5 to 1, and much competition will occur in attempts to secure a mate. In most cases, the largest specimens are successful. Sometimes a large number of males will congregate around a single female, which may even be suffocated in the crush. The male grasps the female around the thoracic region and the pair move about as the female lays a double string of eggs that are fertilized by the male. The eggs may be wound around aquatic plants or other objects in the water. After spawning the females usually leave the water immediately, but the males may stay around for a few days in the hope of procuring another female. Eventually all breeding toads will leave the vicinity of the pond and seek out a terrestrial home until the next breeding season. The eggs hatch

The green toad, Bufo viridis, *is one of the most colorful toads.*

and the tadpoles develop in the usual anuran manner. The young toadlets usually leave the water in mid to late summer, usually coinciding with heavy rainfall. In captivity, these toads are most likely to breed in outdoor enclosures or in unheated greenhouses with a fairly voluminous pond.

Green Toad
Bufo viridis
Family Bufonidae
Length: 10 cm (4 in)
DESCRIPTION: This is an extremely attractive species. Although having a dry, warty skin like *Bufo bufo*, the resemblance ends here. The pale brown or cream background color is broken with a large number of light green to olive blotches, often with darker borders. The attractive coloration of this species and the ease with which it may be kept make it a popular terrarium subject.
NATURAL RANGE: Eastern part of Europe and into central Asia. Also North Africa and the Mediterranean islands.
HABITAT AND HABITS: Usually found in dryish or sandy lowland habitats. Primarily nocturnal and often seen around human habitations. Will enter villages to hunt insects around street lamps and other sources of light. During the day it lies in shallow burrows or under logs, stones, and other ground cover.
CAPTIVE CARE: A large, dry terrarium with a sandy substrate and a shallow dish of water. Logs or broken crocks should be provided for cover. Provide temperatures to 26°C (79°F) during the day, reduced to 15°C (59°F) at night. Will feed on various small invertebrates. Hibernate for two to three months at 4-5°C (39-41°F).

BREEDING: Success is likely to be achieved only in outdoor enclosures or slightly heated greenhouses with a large water area.

American Toad

Bufo americanus
Family Bufonidae
Length: 11 cm (4½ in)
DESCRIPTION: This can be regarded as the American equivalent of the common European toad, which it may superficially resemble. There are several subspecies and closely related species with a great variation of color, which may be uniform brown to brick-red or olive, sometimes with lighter spots and a light stripe down the back.
NATURAL RANGE: The eastern half of North America, from central Canada to the southern states, but not reaching the Gulf coast (where it is replaced by the southern toad, *Bufo terrestris*).

Top view of the American toad, showing the cranial crests and parotoid glands.

HABITAT AND HABITS: Found in a variety of habitats from gardens and parks to heavily forested mountains, wherever there is

A mating pair of Bufo americanus *in amplexus. The male is the smaller animal on top.*

abundant moisture and food insects.

CAPTIVE CARE: As for the common European toad.

BREEDING: As for the common European toad.

RELATED SPECIES: There are several other species of North American toads requiring similar husbandry. These include the western toad, *Bufo boreas*; Great Plains toad, *Bufo cognatus*; American green toad, *Bufo debilis*; Canadian toad, *Bufo hemiophrys*; and the especially wide-ranging and common Woodhouse's toad, *Bufo woodhousei*.

Giant Toad
Bufo marinus
Family Bufonidae
Length: 25 cm (10 in)
DESCRIPTION: Although a typical bufonid apart from its size, this species is widely kept in the terrarium and deserves special mention. It is usually a uniform gray-brown or reddish brown, with a lighter underside. It has enormous parotid glands extending down the sides of the body from just behind the eyes. A milky fluid from the parotid glands is highly toxic and will burn the eyes and mucous membranes and sometimes inflame the skin. The hands should always be washed carefully after handling any amphibian species, especially this one. Dogs or cats that bit a giant toad have been known to die from the effects of this secretion. Although sometimes called the marine toad, this species is not an inhabitant of salt water although it frequently lives near the coast and the tadpoles will grow in brackish water.

NATURAL RANGE: Central America and northern South America. This

Bufo marinus is often called the marine toad, but it is no more marine than any other amphibian.

species has been introduced to many parts of the world, originally as a pest controller, but in some places it has been so successful that it is now a pest in its own right, threatening native fauna that are being displaced by the toad. In Australia, where it was introduced from Hawaii in 1935 to combat pests of sugar cane, it is now a serious threat to many native amphibians and reptilians. Its sale is now prohibited in several states of the U.S.A.

HABITAT AND HABITS: Primarily nocturnal, hiding under cover during the day but coming out at night to hunt invertebrates and

BREEDING: In spite of its popularity as a pet, captive breeding is uncommon. It is only likely to occur in heated greenhouses with a sizable pond.

European Tree Frog
Hyla arborea
Family Hylidae
Length: 5 cm (2 in)
DESCRIPTION: The family Hylidae contains the typical tree frogs that have adhesive toe discs enabling them to climb more efficiently. However, there are many members of the family that are primarily terrestrial and do not possess toe discs. The

Hyla cipoensis is a small striped tree frog from Brazil. Notice the vocal sac of this calling male.

small vertebrates. Often seen on roads at night.

CAPTIVE CARE: A very easy captive, often becoming tame and trusting; many people have allowed these toads the run of the house. In general, it requires a large terrarium with high humidity and a temperature of around 28°C (82°F) during the day, reduced to about 22°C (72°F) at night. Good ventilation and a shallow bathing dish are essential. Food consist of a variety of large invertebrates (earthworms, locusts, cockroaches, moths, etc.) or small vertebrates (small fish and mice). Cannot be trusted with smaller frogs.

European tree frog is a plump little frog with smooth skin. It is usually bright green on the back with a dark stripe running from the eye down the side of the body, but it may change to brown or yellow depending on the mood.

NATURAL RANGE: Most of Europe except for the North, continuing into Asia.

HABITAT AND HABITS: Mainly nocturnal and usually found in well vegetated habitats near water, including trees, bushes, and reed beds. May be found in low vegetation or sometimes high in trees. Will sunbathe in the spring and autumn.

CAPTIVE CARE: Requires a tall

The gray tree frog, Hyla versicolor, *is a common eastern American species.*

terrarium with a tree branch and robust plants or, ideally, can be kept in a heated greenhouse. Should be kept fairly humid, but with good ventilation and a temperature of about 27°C (81°F), reduced to 20°C (68°F) at night. Food consists mainly of flies (various species), but it will also take other small invertebrates. A period of reduced temperature (two months at 10°C or 50°F) in the winter will simulate hibernation.

BREEDING: Breeding is unlikely in the terrarium but possible in the greenhouse if a planted pool is available. Females lay up to 1000 eggs in small clumps.

RELATED SPECIES: The stripeless tree frog, *Hyla meridionalis*, from southern Europe and North Africa, is similar but lacks the stripe along the flanks. Its husbandry also is similar.

Gray Tree Frog
Hyla versicolor
Family Hylidae
Length: 5 cm (2 in)
DESCRIPTION: A moderate size tree frog with large toe pads. The color is greenish or brownish to gray, with darker blotches forming a lichen-like pattern. The undersides of the thighs are bright orange, and there is a white spot under the eye.

NATURAL RANGE: Eastern half of North America, from the Great Lakes region to the Gulf Coast.

HABITAT AND HABITS: Primarily nocturnal, hiding high up in trees during the day. Usually near permanent water.

CAPTIVE CARE: As described for *H. arborea.*

BREEDING: As described for *H. arborea.*

Green Tree Frog
Hyla cinerea
Family Hylidae
Length: 5 cm (2 in)
DESCRIPTION: This tree frog is very similar in appearance to the European tree frog but is more slender and lacks the dark stripe along the side, this being

replaced with a broad white stripe (sharply outlined in dark) along the upper jaw and side of the body.
NATURAL RANGE: Southern and southeastern U.S.A.
HABITAT AND HABITS: Mainly nocturnal. Lives in vegetation near permanent water. Frequently found resting on the underside of large leaves.
CAPTIVE CARE: As described for *H. arborea*.
BREEDING: As described for *H. arborea*.

Pacific Tree Frog
Hyla regilla
Family Hylidae
Length: 4 cm (1¾ in)
DESCRIPTION: A fairly rough skin

than many other tree frogs. Always close to permanent water. Males call from vertical reeds or stems near the water surface.
CAPTIVE CARE: As described for *H. arborea*.
BREEDING: As described for *H. arborea*.

Spring Peeper
Hyla crucifer
Family Hylidae
Length: 3.5 cm (1⅜ in)
DESCRIPTION: This tiny frog is usually reddish brown, but dark brown and gray specimens may occur. It is characterized by a dark X-shaped mark on the back. It has large toe pads.
NATURAL RANGE: Eastern half of North America from mid-Canada

All eastern American naturalists are familiar with the pipping call of the spring peeper, Hyla crucifer.

with color varying from green through light brown to black, often with darker spots. There is a dark stripe through the eye and a dark patch between the eyes.
NATURAL RANGE: Western coastal states of North America, from southern Canada to Baja California.
HABITAT AND HABITS: Mainly nocturnal and more terrestrial

to the Gulf Coast.
HABITAT AND HABITS: Found in wooded areas close to permanent water. The high-pitched whistling call of the male is made from trees and shrubs in or over-hanging water and is recognized as one of the first signs of spring. Primarily nocturnal.
CAPTIVE CARE: As for *H. arborea*, but smaller food items such as

houseflies and lesser houseflies (*Musca* and *Fannia*) and fruitflies (*Drosophila*) will be required.
BREEDING: As described for *H. arborea*.

Squirrel Tree Frog
Hyla squirella
Family Hylidae
Length: 4 cm (1⅝ in)
DESCRIPTION: This species has an enormous variation in body color ranging through various shades of brown and green to yellow, with darker and lighter spots. There is usually a light stripe along the upper jaw and side of the body but not outlined in dark as in *H. cinerea*. Large toe pads. The usual coloration is bright green without spots. Smaller and not as smooth in appearance as *H. cinerea*.
NATURAL RANGE: Southern U.S.A. from southeastern Virginia to eastern Texas.
HABITAT AND HABITS: Wide range of habitats. Adults hide under tree bark, under leaves, in hollow

trees, and under the eaves of houses. Frequently calls before and after rain.
CAPTIVE CARE: An ideal greenhouse subject. Requires a good supply of small invertebrates (houseflies, fruitflies, etc.). Otherwise care as for *H. arborea*.
BREEDING: Most likely to breed in greenhouses with suitable pond areas.
RELATED SPECIES: There are many further *Hyla* species, most of which make excellent subjects for the tall terrarium or the greenhouse. The North American species will usually do well if kept as described for the European tree frog, *Hyla arborea*, but the South and Central American species would usually prefer higher temperatures, more humidity, no hibernation, and bromeliads in the terrarium.

Red-eyed Tree Frog
Agalychnis callidryas
Family Hylidae

Hyla cinerea *is a large and common green tree frog from the southern U.S.A.*

Length: 7.5 cm (3 in)
DESCRIPTION: Although a delicate species and only recommended for experienced frog keepers, this is such a bizarre and beautiful

The bright yellow eyes of this Agalychnis annae *are striking.*

frog that it really cannot be left out of a book about frogs. The body is slender and the limbs extraordinarily thin. The back is light green, while the flanks are banded in sky-blue and cream. Its large eyes are bright red. It has large toe pads.

NATURAL RANGE: Central America.

HABITAT AND HABITS: A totally arboreal species of the rain forests, rarely descending to the ground. Normally moves with a slow, deliberate, stalking action but can jump well if necessary. Primarily nocturnal.

CAPTIVE CARE: Requires a tall planted terrarium, preferably with robust, large-leaved plants such as *Philodendron, Monstera,* or *Ficus* species. Humidity should be high and preferably accomplished with moving water (by using an airlift). In spite of the high humidity, ventilation must be good. The temperature may rise to 28°C (82°F) during the day, reduced to around 20°C (68°F) at night. Feeds on a variety of small invertebrates.

BREEDING: A large terrarium is required for breeding. Mating occurs in the tree canopy. Eggs are laid on leaves overhanging water. The tadpoles drop into the water as they hatch a few days later. After 40-50 days of development, metamorphosis takes place and the tiny froglets take to the trees.

White's Tree Frog
Litoria caerulea
Family Hylidae
Length: 10 cm (4 in)
DESCRIPTION: Sometimes known as

the giant tree frog, this is a large and robust species with a predisposition to obesity manifested in the folds of flesh frequently seen on the body. The

The red-eyed tree frog, Agalychnis callidryas.

color is predominantly green but may change to brown on

occasion; sometimes there are small white spots scattered over the body. Due to their placid disposition and the ease with which they may be kept, they are highly prized terrarium subjects.

NATURAL RANGE: Northeastern part of Australia and southern New Guinea.

HABITAT AND HABITS: Found in a wide variety of habitats. Frequently encountered around human dwellings, where it may lodge near water tanks and cisterns. Mainly nocturnal with a deep, throaty call.

CAPTIVE CARE: Requires a very large, tall terrarium, with hollow branches and robust plants. Humidity should be moderate and

White's tree frog, Litoria caerulea, *commonly looks this fat.*

(68°F) at night. Food consists of larger invertebrates such as crickets, locusts, beetles, cockroaches, and moths.

BREEDING: Only likely to occur in very large terraria or heated greenhouse accommodations. Frogs may be brought into breeding condition by an increase in humidity by intense spraying over several days. Will breed in pools with a depth of about 30 cm (12 in).

Peron's Tree Frog
Litoria peronii
Family Hylidae
Length: 4 cm (1¼ in)
DESCRIPTION: A slender frog with well developed toe pads. Variable in color, ranging through shades of mottled gray and brown with numerous small bright green

ventilation good. Temperatures to 30°C (86°F), but reduced to 20°C

spots. Insides of thighs black and yellow. Underside whitish or

Popular and Interesting Species

yellowish with black markings on throat.

NATURAL RANGE: Southeastern quarter of Australia.

HABITAT AND HABITS: Occurs in a wide variety of habitats, often some distance from water. May be encountered foraging on the ground after rain but is usually confined to trees and shrubs along streams. It is nocturnal and has a long, rattling call.

CAPTIVE CARE: As described for *H. caerulea.*

BREEDING: As described for *H. caerulea.*

Cuban Tree Frog

Osteopilus septentrionalis
Family Hylidae
Length: 10 cm (4 in)

DESCRIPTION: A large, robust tree frog. Usually brown or bronze in color but may sometimes be green. Very large toe pads and powerful hind limbs. The skin of the top of the head is fused to the bone.

NATURAL RANGE: Cuba, but introduced into Florida.

HABITAT AND HABITS: Nocturnal and found in varied habitats. Common around human

In Osteopilus septentrionalis *the skin of the head is fused to the bones of the skull. This species makes an attractive and hardy pet.*

Many of the most colorful tree frogs are rarely imported. This is the Brazilian Hyla punctata.

habitations in some areas, where it hunts insects, spiders, and even other frogs.

CAPTIVE CARE: As described for *H. caerulea*.

BREEDING: As described for *H. caerulea*.

Ornate Chorus Frog
Pseudacris ornata
Family Hylidae
Length: 3.5 cm (1⅜ in)
DESCRIPTION: A small, plump frog, usually reddish brown with a black stripe through the eye and

Pseudacris triseriata *is one of the most common species of chorus frog. Notice the small toe discs.*

Popular and Interesting Species

dark blotches on the side and low on the back. There are no toe pads.

NATURAL RANGE: Southeastern U.S.A.

HABITAT AND HABITS: Found in low vegetation around areas of permanent or temporary water. Mainly nocturnal, living in burrows during the day. The male's voice is a high-pitched metallic "peep."

CAPTIVE CARE: An aqua-terrarium with about two-thirds land and one-third water. Low plant cover on land area. Temperature to 28°C (82°F) during the day, but reduced to around 20°C (68°F) at night. May be fed on a variety of small invertebrates.

BREEDING: Most likely to breed in greenhouses with a reasonably sized pool and a simulated "wet season."

RELATED SPECIES: There are several other North American species in the genus *Pseudacris* that require similar husbandry, including the mountain chorus frog, *Pseudacris brachyphona*; Brimley's chorus frog, *Pseudacris brimleyi*; spotted chorus frog, *Pseudacris clarki*; Strecker's chorus frog, *Pseudacris streckeri*; and the common chorus frog, *Pseudacris triseriata*. The two U.S.A. species of *Acris* are also very similar but are even more terrestrial; they are called cricket frogs.

Ornate Horned Frog or Horned Escuerzo

Ceratophrys ornata
Family Leptodactylidae
Length: 17.5 cm (7 in)

DESCRIPTION: The family Leptodactylidae is large and includes diverse species of anurans, most species confined to the Southern Hemisphere. The ornate horned frog or horned escuerzo, also sometimes called Bell's horned frog, and other members of the genus *Ceratophrys* show a remarkable similarity in appearance and habit to the unrelated African bullfrog, *Pyxicephalus adspersus*. *C. ornata* has a large head and a huge gape. It has relatively short hind legs and possesses a short,

The southern U.S.A. has many species of interesting tree frogs. This is Hyla gratiosa, *the barking tree frog.*

A typical horned frog looks like it is half mouth—and it is. Ceratophrys aurita makes a great pet.

fleshy "horn" over each eye. There are tooth-like bony projections in the lower jaw. It comes in a variety of colors but is usually green with a network of cream lines and a number of reddish spots and patches.

NATURAL RANGE: The Argentine pampas and adjacent areas of South America.

HABITAT AND HABITS: A burrowing species brought into activity by heavy rains. Has an enormous appetite and can overpower and swallow creatures almost its own size, including other frogs and mice.

CAPTIVE CARE: A dry terrarium with a large water dish and areas into which the frog can burrow. Only single specimens should be kept unless they are of similar size (and even then it may be dangerous to try). Temperatures should be no higher than 27°C (81°F) during the day, reduced somewhat at night.

BREEDING: Breeding may occur in heated greenhouses with a suitable pond and a simulated "wet season." The tadpoles are as carnivorous as the adults.

Water Holding Frog

Cyclorana platycephalus
Family Leptodactylidae
Length: 6 cm (2½ in)
DESCRIPTION: A round, plump frog with a flat head and the eyes set prominently upward. May be dull olive-gray to green or gray with light green patches. There is often

a narrow light green vertical stripe. The underside is whitish.

NATURAL RANGE: The drier inland regions of Australia.

HABITAT AND HABITS: A burrowing species that is only active when conditions are humid after heavy rains. It is able to estivate for long periods in very dry areas by burrowing deep into the soil and making a cocoon-like chamber with an impervious lining that is filled with water. Aboriginal natives used to exploit this desert water source.

CAPTIVE CARE: A large dry terrarium with facilities for burrowing. The frog will not estivate if kept supplied with permanent water. Feeds on a variety of invertebrates. It may be kept at a temperature of around 28°C (82°F), reduced somewhat at night.

BREEDING: No records of captive breeding have been found, but experimentation with dry periods and artificial rainfall would appear to be the best course to take.

RELATED SPECIES: There are a number of other Australian species in the genus with similar habits, including the large *Cyclorana australis*, a burrowing frog that grows to 10 cm (4 in).

Although there are hundreds of species of Eleutherodactylus, *they are seldom available and are too small for most hobbyists.*

Whistling Frog

Eleutherodactylus johnstonei
Family Leptodactylidae
Length: 2 cm (¾ in)

DESCRIPTION: This tiny frog is just an example of the over 400 very similar species in the genus. It is usually reddish brown with darker markings on the back.

NATURAL RANGE: The island of Jamaica.

HABITAT AND HABITS: A terrestrial species found in humid mossy undergrowth.

CAPTIVE CARE: Provide a relatively small terrarium with a mossy floor covering and high humidity. Although not strictly necessary, a small water dish is recommended to help maintain humidity. The temperature may be kept at 23-26°C (73-79°F) day and night. Food consists of various small invertebrates.

BREEDING: This species and other members of the genus are interesting in that they complete their life cycles without a free-swimming larval stage. The eggs are laid in damp mossy areas, and the complete development of the tadpole takes place inside the relatively large outer membrane from which the fully metamorphosed froglets emerge after a few weeks. A few species have taken this to an extreme,

central New South Wales and southern Queensland.

HABITAT AND HABITS: A burrowing species especially abundant on the flood plains of the large river system. After heavy rain, it breeds in temporary pools.

CAPTIVE CARE: Provide a dry terrarium with burrowing facilities. The temperature can reach 30°C (86°F) during the day, reduced to around 20°C (68°F) at night. There should be a general temperature reduction in winter.

Physalaemus nattereri is an oddly patterned leptodactylid from the Amazon.

holding the eggs and tadpoles in the body and giving live birth to fully developed froglets.

Crucifix Toad

Notaden bennettii
Family Leptodactylidae
Length: 5 cm (2 in)
DESCRIPTION: This remarkable little anuran may be olive, green, or bright yellow above with shiny black and red warts in the form of a cross on the back. The underside is white.
NATURAL RANGE: Australia, in

The food is mainly ants, but other small invertebrates are also taken.

BREEDING: No records of captive breeding could be found, but simulated rainfall will no doubt be worth experimenting with.

RELATED SPECIES: Related but not quite so spectacularly colored species in the genus include the northern Australian spadefoot toad, *Notaden melanoscaphus*, and the desert Australian spadefoot toad, *Notaden nichollsi*.

Suggested Reading

ENCYCLOPEDIA OF REPTILES AND AMPHIBIANS
By John F. Breen
ISBN 0-87666-220-3
TFH H-935

Contents: Turtles Common And Rare. Other Turtles And The Tortoises. Alligators, Caimans, And Crocodiles. Native American Lizards. Exotic Lizards And The Tuatara. Harmless North American Snakes. Non-Poisonous Exotic Snakes. Poisonous Snakes. Newts, Salamanders And Caecilians. Frogs And Toads. Collecting Herptiles. Feeding A Collection. Illnesses And Other Problems.

Audience: This book is an enormous coverage of the care, collection and identification of reptiles and amphibians. Written for either the amateur or professional.
Hard cover, 5½ x 8", 576 pages
316 black and white photos, 267 color photos

BREEDING TERRARIUM ANIMALS
By Elke Zimmermann
H-1078

In *Breeding Terrarium Animals* the author presents her experiences and those of her colleagues in condensed but very readable form filled with information of use to hobbyists and professional herpetologists alike. Profusely illustrated in color, the book covers almost 100 species in detail, with basic information on dozens more. For the main species there are discussions of care, identification, and distribution, followed by detailed observations on the breeding behavior, incubation, and care of the young. The other species are grouped with the major species by their similarity in breeding behavior and listed with such essentials as number of eggs, incubation period, and temperature preference. In total, almost 350 species are covered, from axolotls to *Xenopus* among the amphibians and agamas to *Xantusia* among the reptiles. The discussions of the complicated life histories of the fascinating poison arrow frogs (*Dendrobates* and *Phyllobates*) are especially detailed. Good discussions of general terrarium maintenance, rearing food animals, and methods of egg incubation round out the book.
Hard cover; 6 x 9", 384 pages
Contains over 175 full-color photos

Index

Green poison arrow frogs are among the most gaudily colored of all the frogs. Like all Dendrobates, they are delicate if not kept under perfect conditions.

CO-041 S

FROGS & TOADS

A COMPLETE INTRODUCTION

Horned frogs have become very popular lately as they have a distinct personality (vicious and aggressive) and are easy to care for. This is Ceratophrys ornata.